COOKING WITH WINE

'Use a little wine for thy stomach's sake.' (I Timothy 5:23)

AUGUSTUS BARNETT'S

Cooking with Wine

EDITED BY

DERECK WILLIAMS

With an introduction by Brian Barnett

ELM TREE BOOKS

HAMISH HAMILTON · LONDON

First published in Great Britain 1973
by Elm Tree Books Ltd
90 Great Russell Street London WC1

SBN 241 02275 4

Illustrations by Patricia Clements
Photographs by Angel Studio
Accessories by Harvey Nichols of Knightsbridge

Printed in Great Britain by
Western Printing Services Ltd, Bristol

Contents

Introduction

MY FATHER Augustus Barnett was a chef at a leading London hotel for thirty-six years but when I left school I decided to join a firm of chartered accountants as an articled clerk. I was called up two years later, served in the RAF as an accounts clerk, and after demobilisation I became a salesman. I was quite good at it—I never starved and was never fired. But I never saved anything either and when I met Leslie Clark, at that time working in an off-licence in Stanmore, I discovered that we shared a common interest, that of making money.

Leslie, now my Managing Director, subsequently met Leslie Bricusse, whose music for the West End hit *Stop the World—I Want to Get Off* had already made him a rich man. We got on well with Bricusse, so with our know-how and his financial backing we started a restaurant in North London.

I soon realised that there wasn't enough return from the business at that stage to support us all, so then I hit upon the idea of selling wines by mail order. There was no risk because it was all cash-with-order business. Nor did I hold any stocks, for as the mail came in, I would rush round the corner and buy the necessary wine. I bought a small hand press for £8 and then printed the labels, which included the customer's name—a great gimmick. I worked at home for three years and then decided to buy an off-licence.

This was in 1966, by which time I had become friends with one of the wine-importing companies. With their backing, I was able to raise cash and set myself up in my first shop, formerly a run-down dairy in Penge, South London. Luckily the dairy held a licence to sell liquor.

Although my original plan was to continue with the 'own

label' sales, such was the pressure of business from local customers that I decided to change my tactics. My stock was always cheap because the suppliers allowed me a whole month's credit, so I had to sell it within that time in order to raise the cash to pay their account. Nevertheless, I was able to cut prices to a minimum, and this policy was so successful that I found it essential to expand. The business exploded quickly and I was taking £1,000 a week before I even bought a till.

At this time, in need of help, I sent an SOS to my friend Leslie Clark whose restaurant had just closed after four years, crippled by the government restrictions on expense-account eating. He had been running the restaurant extremely successfully and had achieved the distinction of gaining the highest food/comfort/service rating from Egon Ronay in North London. Meals were served with wines from a particular wine-growing district, and the district changed every week so that the food served was typical of the region featured. Charging from £4 to £7 per head, and shopping at the most exclusive food stores, he seemed to have found the formula for success. In 1964, Leslie started his 'Gourmet Club', which at first met monthly, but eventually became so popular that he decided to reserve every Monday for the club meetings. Gradually he persuaded his regular members to become customers.

However, since the restaurant had closed, Leslie was able to come to my aid just in time for the Christmas rush.

Our next move was to take a lease on two more off-licences in Hastings and Portsmouth. At this stage we had to rely on the goodwill I had built up with my suppliers to persuade them to wait for their money, because all the takings had to be chanelled into paying for the buildings. We took a great risk, in committing everything to expansion, but it was one which paid off.

Today, our formula of giving the public all the alcohol it wants at rock-bottom prices is unbeatable. We offer an unrivalled selection of 700 different wines and spirits at all our shops, from Château Lafite 1881 at £49 a bottle, to a Spanish Sauterne at 46p. Fast sales and low overheads enable us to cut costs to a minimum, and we are well enough established now to buy in bulk at the most advantageous prices, which are then passed on to the customers.

I have learnt a good deal about wines over the years, and now feel that my experience and knowledge can profitably be passed on to others, together with the wealth of information concerning food which we have both gained in our restaurant experience, and which has also been passed on to me by my father. All of this has been incorporated in what we hope will prove an invaluable book—*Cooking with Wine*.

BRIAN BARNETT,
Chairman,
Augustus Barnett & Son Limited

Cooking with Wine

DESPITE THE vicissitudes of fashion, which exerts as great an influence over our eating habits as it does upon our taste in clothes, there will always be certain time-honoured dishes revered throughout the world of international cuisine. With the recent burgeoning of foreign restaurants in this country and the increased availability of holidays abroad, it is not surprising that people have grown to enjoy a correspondingly wide range of food and wine. For those who wish to reproduce in their own homes dishes they have enjoyed elsewhere, the recipes in this book will prove useful.

Many of these dishes, British and foreign alike, require the addition of wine—the right wine, in the right quantity—to give them the unique and unforgettable flavour which has established and maintained their popularity over the years. Some recipes, among them Boeuf Bourguignon, may be left to simmer slowly on the top of the cooker, which is one reason why so many professional chefs include them on their menus. Others are very quick to prepare and require very little effort, but that all-important liquid additive can put them in the *cordon bleu* class.

When wine is added to food, a subtle chemical reaction takes place which can improve the food's flavour, texture, and digestibility, but it need not, as many housewives erroneously imagine, add a great deal to the cost of the meal. The following facts bear this out:

(1) The glycerin and tannin in wine help to mix food together in our stomachs. Thus there is no foundation for the view that dishes based on wine are difficult to digest.

(2) The alcohol in wine gives a special flavour to the other ingredients and brings out the taste of ingredients or dishes that

are otherwise insipid. So again, it is not true to maintain that recipes based on wine are expensive: often, the use of wine makes it possible for cheaper cuts of meat to be used.

(3) As a moistening agent in most dishes, wine allows you to cut down on the amount of fat you need for cooking—especially since the amount of glycerin in wine is from 4–20 grams (it varies from one type to another). The recipes in this book allow for this, so do not add extra fat to any of them. If you need to pre-cook the meat slightly, you can do it in a very small amount of butter or oil in a different pan.

WINE IN COOKING

What sort of wine should I use?

It would of course be both ridiculous and misleading to give any hard and fast rules: ridiculous because eating is, after all, a matter of taste, which cannot be dictated, and misleading because, with a few exceptions (particularly in fish dishes), recipes based on wine are flexible and can easily be adapted. There are, of course, 'basic recipes', but these can be varied in any way you fancy.

Remember that unless you're obliged to produce a real banquet you certainly don't have to use the best vintage wines (i.e. classed growths, the aristocrats of the wine-growing areas)—or even medium vintage wines, for cooking. If you're lucky enough to have some, you would do better to keep them for drinking! For cooking, use a genuine regional wine or a pleasant wine bottled within the year (which, believe me, is what the greatest chefs use), and avoid taking risks by asking for reliably branded wines.

One word of warning: if you have a little vintage wine left over, do not make the mistake of pouring it onto whatever you are cooking at the last minute. Instead, use it for the actual cooking and make it go further if necessary by adding another less 'noble' wine of the same type. For instance, if you have a little Clos de Vougeot left, complement it with some Juliénas or Beaujolais (in other words, two different Burgundies: it is always better not to mix aromas).

'Mature', 'heady', 'full-bodied', 'balanced', 'fruity': many and various are the terms used to describe wine. In this book we have endeavoured to emphasise the different qualities and properties of wine, and the part it plays in what might be called 'culinary alchemy'.

It does not matter in the least whether you use red, white or rosé wine, young or old, sparkling, recently bottled or vintage, French or otherwise. Although you will find that one or two recipes *do* specify a particular wine, the great majority can be adapted according to your taste. If you wish, you can prepare a court-bouillon using red wine, or even a fish soup '*au vin blanc*' with red. Similarly, the quantities stated in each list of ingredients can be varied to taste.

Can I use real 'plonk', or wines that are 'below par'?
No, do not use plonk, sour wine, wine from a barrel or corked wine, flat or 'weak' wine (i.e. wine that is too old and has therefore lost all its bouquet) in cooking. It may evaporate completely during cooking, or if not, it will certainly not enhance the dish.

What are the general regional variations?
Wine is obtained from the fermentation of fresh grapes, the sugar in which is transformed into alcohol by the yeast in the fermenting process. Because the vine reacts to climatic conditions, the wines from the south will be naturally rather strong, whereas wines produced in northern climes will have more subtle flavours.

Is wine a beneficial addition to the diet?
Wine contains mineral salts (magnesium, phosphorus, chlorine, fluorine, zinc, trace elements), vitamins B1 and B2 and even a small amount of iron. Provided you do not drink too much of it, wine may be considered both nourishing and mineralising. In dishes cooked with wine the glycerin, the ether in the 'bouquet' and the tannin, which are activated by cooking, are beneficial for those who suffer from dyspepsia and for those whose digestion is rather slow.

What are blended wines, and what about wines labelled VDQS?
Blended wines: varieties from different vineyards can be mixed

together in such a way that a top-quality wine is obtained. But these wines can give you a nasty surprise, so trust only well-known names which have a reputation to keep up: use branded blended wines to avoid costly errors. In order to protect both guaranteed vintages and local wines, blended and branded wines, French law prohibits the use of the terms *château*, *clos*, *domaine*, *moulin*, *côte*, *cru*, *monopole* or any other word likely to confuse the buyer on anything other than guaranteed vintages (*appellations contrôlées*).

The 'VDQS' label means that there's no question of a nasty surprise. The trademark printed with these initials and the words '*Vin délimité de qualité supérieure*' is generally well displayed on the label. French law is very strict about guarantee-labelling and all references to VDQS are subject to the governmental decree which requires producers to maintain the quality of any wine labelled thus.

Canapés, Soups and Starters

THIS SECTION includes canapés, for serving at parties, and soups and starters, to set the tone of the meal. If lack of time prevents you preparing your own homemade soup, it is worth remembering that a large variety of soups (whether homemade, tinned or packeted) will have a better flavour if a little wine is added either at the end of the cooking time or when reheating them. For example, here are some suggestions for wine additions to several different kinds of soup:

Beef and oxtail broth (red wine)
Chicken or other poultry broth (white wine)
Lobster, crab or crawfish bisque (dry white wine)
Fish soup (red or white wine)
French onion soup with bread (white wine)
Cream of mushroom soup (a few drops of white wine).

Note: the wine must always be warmed before being stirred into the soup.

The colloquial French word for soups made with wine is *chabrot*, and it is common in France to see diners pour red wine into the bottom of their soup plates and mop up the rich liquid with large chunks of bread!

Frankfurters with Cheese Dip

4 tablespoons dry white wine
cocktail frankfurters
½ pound processed sliced cheese
1 teaspoon prepared mustard
1 teaspoon Worcestershire sauce

Melt the cheese in a double boiler and blend in the wine and seasonings.

Note: Large frankfurters may be used cut into suitable pieces. The quantities given above make enough dip for three cans of frankfurters.

Flavoured Cheese Spread

½ pint dry or medium sherry
½ pound grated Cheddar cheese
½ pound blue cheese (crumbled)
salt and onion salt to taste
3 ounces cream cheese
¾ teaspoon Worcestershire sauce
½ teaspoon paprika
dash of garlic powder

Put the cheeses in a bowl and blend well with a fork. Beat in the sherry gradually. Add the seasonings and beat until smooth and creamy.

Excellent for canapés, and keeps well.

Edam Dip

4 tablespoons dry French vermouth, or *Italian dry vermouth*
½ pound Edam cheese
a generous teaspoon Worcestershire sauce
½ teaspoon prepared mustard
onion salt to taste
garlic salt to taste

Grate the cheese. Blend in the wine and add the remainder of the ingredients. Serve in a bowl surrounded with an assortment of dry biscuits.

Blue Cheese Spread or Dip

4 tablespoons dry red or *white wine*
½ pound blue cheese
6 ounces cream cheese
pinch of garlic powder
salt to taste
1 tablespoon mayonnaise
¼ teaspoon paprika
½ teaspoon Worcestershire sauce
pinch of cayenne

Crumble the blue cheese and blend in the cream cheese. Beat in the wine and mayonnaise. Add the seasonings and mix well.

This can be used as a spread or as a dip for potato crisps.

Scampi Dip

4 tablespoons medium sherry
½ pint mayonnaise
1 tablespoon grated onion
salt to taste
2 tablespoons chopped parsley
1 teaspoon Worcestershire sauce
5 tablespoons chilli sauce

Mix all ingredients and chill thoroughly. When ready to serve, spear the scampi with toothpicks, and arrange around the bowl containing the dip.

Cheese of the Seven Herbs

3 tablespoons sherry
4 ounces grated cheese
2 level tablespoons of the following herbs:
finely chopped parsley
sage
thyme
tarragon
chives
chervil
winter savory
seasoning to taste

Put all the ingredients into a double saucepan and stir over very gentle heat until the mixture is creamy and pale green in colour. While still warm, fill up small pots with the cheese and use when cold.

Cheese and Bacon Canapés

4 tablespoons dry or medium sherry
½ pound Cheddar cheese
2 egg yolks
4 rashers bacon
½ teaspoon Worcestershire sauce
salt
cayenne
12 slices bread

Blend the cheese and sherry; stir in the egg yolks, slightly beaten; add salt and cayenne. Cut each rasher of bacon into 6 or 8 pieces, and cook until nearly crisp. Toast the bread on one side only and spread the untoasted side with the cheese mixture. Cut each into four pieces and place a piece of bacon on each. Grill slowly until the cheese mixture becomes puffy and the bacon is crisp. Serve at once.

Cheese Dip

2 tablespoons medium sherry
1 packet cream cheese (about 2 ounces)
equal quantity of blue cheese
salt
1 tablespoon mayonnaise
1 tablespoon whipped cream
horseradish sauce
½ teaspoon Worcestershire sauce

Mix the two cheeses with a fork. Add the mayonnaise and the horseradish sauce to taste and stir well. Put in the Worcestershire sauce, the salt and the sherry. Blend all well together.

Shrimp Canapés

1 tablespoon dry red wine
2 tablespoons cream cheese
shrimps
2 tablespoons peanut butter
1 teaspoon curry powder
good pinch of salt

Blend well together the cream cheese, peanut butter, curry powder, salt and red wine. When thoroughly mixed spread on suitable dry biscuits and put a shrimp on each.

Cheese Spread

5 tablespoons dry white wine
1 pound grated Gruyère cheese
1 clove garlic
3½ tablespoons butter
5 tablespoons water
salt and pepper

Cook the cheese with the butter, wine, water, and the garlic chopped very fine. Season with salt and pepper. Stir continually over a low heat until the mixture is smooth and creamy. Pour into an earthenware bowl and leave to cool.

Chestnut Soup

½ pint Madeira	*1 onion*
2 pounds chestnuts	*1 stalk celery*
2 tablespoons butter	*1 pint consommé*
½ pint cooking oil	*1½ pints chicken broth*
1 carrot	*½ pint scalded cream*
salt and pepper	*dry mustard*

To prepare chestnuts make two crisscross cuts on the flat side with a pointed knife. Heat about ½ pint cooking oil in a large frying pan, add the chestnuts and let them heat over high heat for 5 minutes or so, at the same time shaking the pan and stirring the chestnuts. Drain them and leave them until they are cool enough to handle. With a sharp knife remove the shell and skin.

Put the butter in a saucepan with the peeled and sliced onion, sliced carrot and the stalk of celery cut up. Sauté for about 10 minutes, but do not brown. Add the peeled and skinned chestnuts, salt and pepper and the consommé. Simmer gently until the chestnuts are soft (about 25 minutes). Into the same pan strain the consommé and rub the chestnuts and vegetables through a sieve. Add the chicken broth and bring to the boil. Now stir in the scalded cream seasoned with a pinch of dry mustard and salt. Bring to the boil once more. Remove from the heat and add the Madeira.

Curried Chicken Soup

3 tablespoons sherry	*½ pint thick cream*
2 cans condensed chicken soup	*2 teaspoons curry powder*
½ can consommé	*½ raw apple*

Heat the chicken soup and the consommé in the top of a double boiler. Add the sherry and the cream, stirring slowly. Add the curry powder, stirring well. After the soup has been put into the soup bowls, sprinkle the top with the raw apple finely diced.

Fish Soup

1½ pints dry white wine
4½ pounds small fish (soles, plaice, or eels, cut into pieces)
12 average-sized onions
8 ounces butter
1 clove garlic
large bouquet garni
3 cloves
salt and pepper

Cut the onions into quarters and put them into a large earthenware casserole with the butter, garlic, bouquet garni, cloves, salt and pepper. Add the fish, cover with the wine and boil for 30 to 45 minutes. When the fish are done, remove from the casserole and keep hot. Reduce the cooking liquor by half, then pour over the fish. Potatoes may be added to the above recipe by cooking them in the soup, whole, at the same time as the fish.

Cream of Mushroom Soup

½ gill white wine
8 ounces mushrooms
2 slices onion
1 quart chicken or veal stock
2 ounces butter
1 ounce flour
¼ pint milk
¼ pint cream
salt and pepper to taste

Peel and slice the mushrooms into a saucepan. Add the onion and stock. Cover and simmer gently for 20 minutes. Rub through a sieve. Melt the butter. Add the flour. Stir till frothy. Draw the pan to the side of the stove and stir in the milk. Return to the stove and stir until boiling. Boil for 3 or 4 minutes, stirring constantly. Add mushroom purée. Stir till boiling. Heat cream slightly. Stir into soup. Season with salt and pepper to taste, then stir in the wine. When piping hot, serve garnished with whipped cream.

Cream of Corn Soup

Madeira or *sherry to taste*
1 large slice of onion
2 pints hot milk
1 medium-sized can of sweet corn
1 pint white stock
1 ounce butter
1 ounce flour
salt and pepper to taste
whipped cream

Place the onion in a saucepan and add the milk. Bring to boiling point. Draw pan to side of stove and leave for 30 minutes. Remove onion. Add corn to the stock and pour into a saucepan. Cover. Simmer gently for 20 minutes, then rub through a sieve. Melt the butter. Stir in flour and when frothy gradually stir in two-thirds of the milk. Stir till boiling then add remainder of milk. Cook, stirring constantly, till smooth and thick. Stir into corn purée, then reheat. Season to taste. Flavour to taste with the wine. Serve in bouillon cups. Float a teaspoon of whipped cream on each portion.

Clear Soup (Consommé)

½ gill Madeira or *sherry*
2 quarts beef stock
8 ounces shin of beef
1 medium-sized onion
1 medium-sized carrot
1 stick celery
1 tablespoon cold water
2 egg whites
small piece of bay leaf
2 whole cloves
12 black peppercorns
1 sprig marjoram
1 sprig thyme

Carefully remove all fat from the stock. Chop the meat finely or put through a mincer. Peel and slice the onion. Scrape and slice the carrot and celery. Place the vegetables in a large saucepan. Stir in stock, stiffly frothed egg whites, two crushed egg shells, bay leaf, cloves, peppercorns, marjoram and thyme. Place pan on stove. Beat contents with an egg whisk until the mixture comes to the boil. Simmer slowly for 10 minutes then add the wine. Bring to boiling point. Remove from stove. Stand for

5 minutes. Pour into a jelly bag and allow the soup to drip into a basin below. Rinse saucepan, add soup and reheat. Add a lump of sugar and salt and pepper to taste.

Consommé Fitzroy

1 glass sherry
1½ pints chicken and veal consommé (with little onion, oregano, basil and seasoning)
¼ pound cooked ox tongue
¼ pound tapioca
1 can asparagus tips

Make a consommé with chicken and veal, a little onion, carrot, oregano, basil and season to taste. Cut the tongue into strips and the asparagus tips in half. Put the consommé into a saucepan and bring to the boil. Add the tapioca and simmer for about 15 minutes. Now put in the asparagus tips, the juice from the can, the wine and the tongue. Place on high heat for a few moments and season to taste.

Cold Cherry Soup

2 gills sweet white wine
2¼ pounds fresh cherries
1 stick cinnamon
½ pound castor sugar
¼ pint cream
2 pints water
2 ounces blanched almonds
4 teaspoons cornflour

Skin the almonds, cut in strips and toast lightly. Wash and stem 2 pounds of the cherries and put in a saucepan with the water and cinnamon stick and boil for 25 minutes. In the meantime, stone the remaining cherries and put aside for the garnish. Strain the juice from the cooked cherries into a saucepan, add the sugar and bring to the boil. Add the stoned cherries. Mix the cornflour with half a cup of water and thicken the soup slightly. Whisk well to avoid lumps. Boil for about 2 minutes, remove from the heat and add the wine. Serve cold in soup cups with a spoonful of whipped cream on each portion and sprinkle with the toasted almonds.

Pâté

a little Madeira
½ pound chicken livers
6 tablespoons chicken fat
1 large onion
salt and pepper
thyme

Sauté the sliced onion in half of the hot chicken fat until golden brown. Then, in another pan, sauté the chicken livers in the remainder of the hot fat for about 5 minutes, to which a little thyme has been added, add salt and pepper to taste. Now put the mixed chicken livers and onion through a mincer and mince as finely as possible. When cool add enough Madeira to make to the consistency of pâté.

Liver Pâté

1 tablespoon sherry
½ pound liver sausage
3 ounces cream cheese
1 tablespoon Worcestershire sauce
½ pint double cream
1 tablespoon melted butter
salt
pepper
curry powder

Blend together the liver sausage and cream cheese. Add the cream, melted butter, Worcestershire sauce and sherry; salt and pepper to taste. Add the curry powder a pinch at a time until the flavour pleases you.

Fish Cocktail

3 tablespoons Madeira or *sherry*
1½ cups prepared fish
2½ tablespoons tarragon vinegar
salt and cayenne pepper to taste
juice of 1 lemon
¼ pint tomato ketchup
1 teaspoon Worcestershire sauce

Use 1½ cups flaked crab, diced lobster, shelled prawns or shrimps, or 2½ dozen small oysters. Chill fish thoroughly. Mix remaining ingredients together in the order given. Chill. Divide equally between 6 fish cocktail glasses, or fruit glasses, lined with crisp heart of lettuce. Serve with hot cheese straws.

Smoked Salmon Salad

3 tablespoons claret
2 ounces smoked salmon
6 anchovy fillets
3 cold boiled potatoes
1 ounce Gruyère cheese
1 sweet pickled gherkin
1 cored peeled apple
1 crisp lettuce heart
4 tablespoons Sauce Tartare
2 tablespoons mayonnaise
1 stick celery

Cut the salmon in dice. Chop the anchovy fillets, preserved in oil, potatoes and cheese. Mince the gherkin. Chop the apple, lettuce heart and celery. Mix all these ingredients together, then stir in the claret. Cover and stand for 5 minutes. Stir in the Sauce Tartare and mayonnaise. Serve as a course, in mixed hors d'oeuvres, or as a single hors d'oeuvres garnished with prawns, slices of hard-boiled egg and watercress.

Stuffed Avocado Pears

6 tablespoons Madeira or *brown sherry*
3 ripe avocado pears
1½ pounds Muscatel grapes
lemon juice (as required)

Halve the pears lengthways, then carefully remove the large stones. Brush the insides freely with lemon juice to prevent discoloration, then chill. Halve the grapes lengthways and carefully remove the seeds. Pile into the pear halves. Sprinkle each portion with a tablespoon of the wine.

Baked Avocado

1 gill Madeira
3 avocado pears
1 tablespoon oil
½ tablespoon tarragon vinegar
parsley (finely chopped)
½ tablespoon chives (finely chopped)
salt and pepper

Cut the avocado pears lengthways in half. Remove the stones. Place on a baking sheet and fill the halves with the wine. Place in a low oven to bake slowly for 20 minutes. Mix the oil, vinegar, chives and parsley, and the seasoning. Fill the baked pears with the mixture and serve.

Risotto Milanaise

4 tablespoons white wine
1 pound rice
1–2 onions
4 ounces butter
saffron
6 ounces grated cheese
2 ounces beef marrow
1½ pints of good beef or *chicken stock*
salt and pepper

Put the butter and the beef marrow into a deep frying pan, and when hot add the chopped onion and cook till it begins to brown. Then add the rice, stir well, and cook for 15 minutes. Add the boiling stock, the white wine, a good pinch of saffron, salt and pepper, and mix all well together. Simmer gently for 20–30 minutes, stirring occasionally. Just before serving, sprinkle with the grated cheese and 2 ounces melted butter.

Hot Grapefruit

1 glass white wine
3 grapefruit
2 tablespoons redcurrant jelly
6 tablespoons castor sugar
6 black olives
dash of cayenne pepper

Cut the grapefruit in halves, remove inside skin and seeds and cut into sections. Put on a dish and sprinkle each half with a teaspoon of sugar. Place under the grill or in a hot oven until heated through. Melt the redcurrant jelly with the wine and a dash of cayenne pepper, bring to the boil and glaze the grapefruit with the mixture. Place a black olive in the centre of each grapefruit half. Excellent served with poultry or game.

Egg Dishes

PROTEIN-PACKED, quick-to-cook egg dishes can either replace the fish course of a main meal or be served as snacks or light lunches, so check the number of servings given in accordance with your own requirements. Egg dishes, and especially omelettes, should be served immediately they are cooked (unless hard-boiled).

Puffy Omelette

3 tablespoons white wine
8 eggs
4 tablespoons butter
2 teaspoons chopped shallots
3 chicken livers cut into 4 pieces each
4 medium mushrooms (coarsely chopped)
salt and pepper
½ pint milk
⅛ teaspoon salt
12 small mushroom caps (sautéed)
1 teaspoon chopped parsley

In a medium skillet, melt 2 tablespoons butter and add shallots. Cook, stirring, for 1 minute, or until soft. Add chicken livers and mushrooms, sprinkle with salt and pepper. Cook gently until liver is done. Do not overcook. Add dry white wine and cook, stirring, for 2–3 minutes. Use as filling for omelette. Break eggs into a large bowl. Add ⅛ teaspoon salt and beat with a large wire whisk or electric beater until very frothy. Add milk and beat again until frothy. Melt 2 tablespoons of butter in a very large skillet over high heat. When butter is hot, but not smoking, pour in omelette mixture. Cover, keep on high heat for 15 seconds, then quickly reduce heat to very low and cook for 8–10 minutes. Peek under lid. Eggs should have puffed up and have a smooth satiny look. If they haven't puffed up, continue cooking. When eggs are done, spread the sauce over one half. Using a suitable spatula, carefully fold other half over sauce. Turn omelette onto a large warm platter. Garnish with sautéed mushroom caps and sprinkle with chopped parsley.

Serves 4

Eggs in Aspic

2 tablespoons dry French vermouth
4 eggs, poached and cooled (reserve and crush 2 shells)
4 cups strong chicken broth, room temperature
6 thin slices ham (cut into ovals)
2 good pinches tarragon
2 teaspoons lemon juice
1 egg white
2 envelopes unflavoured gelatin
4 stuffed olives

Add tarragon, lemon juice, and wine to chicken broth. Beat in egg white and crushed egg shells. Bring to the boil and strain through a clean, wet, finely woven cotton cloth or several layers of cheese-cloth which have been rinsed in hot water. Remove ½ cup broth, cool quickly. Dissolve gelatin in it. Stir remaining hot broth into gelatin mixture. Heat until gelatin is completely dissolved. Chill until syrupy but still liquid.

Slice olives. Spoon a thin layer of gelatin mixture into bottom of four cup-shaped moulds. Chill until firm. Arrange stuffed olive slices into desired pattern and cover with another layer of gelatin mixture. Chill until firm.

Trim poached eggs with round pastry cutter or paring knife. Place 1 egg in each mould and cover with layer of chilled, syrupy gelatin mixture until not quite full. Place a slice of ham on each mould and cover with a layer of remaining aspic. Chill for several hours, or until quite firm. Unmould on to serving dish. Garnish as desired with watercress, capers, and/or mayonnaise.

Serves 4

Sole with Black and Green Grapes (*page* 37)

Ham Baked in Port (*page* 57)

Eggs and Chicken Livers Baked in Madeira

1 gill Madeira	*salt and pepper*
6 eggs	*butter*
¾ pound chicken livers	*¾ gill cream*

Sauté the chicken livers in the butter for about 8 minutes. Add salt and pepper to taste. Beat the eggs together with the cream and Madeira. Butter a casserole and pour in the eggs and chicken livers. Cover and bake in a slow oven for approximately 25 minutes. Serve hot.

Serves 4–6

Eggs Poached in Wine and Mushroom Soup

dry white wine	*salt*
2 eggs	*pepper*
1 can condensed cream of mushroom soup	*slices of buttered toast*

Empty the contents of a tin of mushroom soup into a shallow saucepan. Add enough dry white wine to make it of the consistency of sauce. Heat over a low flame until the liquid simmers. Break two eggs into the sauce, add salt and pepper. Cover the pan and simmer for about 3 minutes, or until the whites of the eggs are set. Remove the eggs carefully on to slices of buttered toast and pour the sauce over them.

Serves 2

Eggs in White Wine Sauce

1 bottle white wine	*1 clove garlic*
6 eggs	*3½ ounces little white onions*
3½ ounces streaky bacon (chopped into small pieces)	*6 croûtons*
	thyme
3½ ounces mushrooms	*bay leaf*

Make a court-bouillon (see page 118 for method) with the white wine, thyme, bay leaf and clove of garlic. Poach the eggs in the court-bouillon, drain and put in a warm place. Boil down the court-bouillon. Then lightly fry the bacon pieces, sauté the mushrooms and brown the little onions (separately). Fry the croûtons until golden brown. Place the eggs on the croûtons. Strain the sauce, add the bacon, onions and mushrooms, and pour it over the eggs.

Serves 4–6

Double Spanish Omelette

1 glass sherry
8 eggs (4 for each omelette)
spinach
chives
tomatoes
butter
garlic
parsley
lean cooked ham
mushrooms
tomato sauce
yolk of egg

Make two omelettes: colour one a bright green by mixing with the omelette a little spinach, previously boiled then sautéed in butter and rubbed through a sieve, and chopped chives.

Blend the other omelette in the same way but with tomato pulp and skin, sautéed in butter, with garlic and a little chopped parsley, and rubbed through a sieve; this produces a red omelette. Fry the chopped ham and mushrooms in a little butter, with chopped parsley. Moisten with the sherry and a little stock.

Put the green omelette on a hot dish without folding. Spread over it the ham and mushrooms and over this place the red omelette. Serve with a tomato sauce to which the yolk of an egg and a little butter have been added.

Serves 6

Anchovy Eggs

1 tablespoon Marsala
salt and white pepper to taste
6 anchovy fillets
½ gill jellied stock
6 eggs

Butter 6 small ramekins. Sprinkle the dishes with salt and pepper. Chop fillets finely and place in a saucepan. Add stock and wine. Boil for 5 minutes. Break an egg into each ramekin. Sprinkle with paprika. Divide the sauce evenly between the dishes. Bake in a moderate oven (350°F./Gas 4) until the eggs are set (about 5 minutes).

Serves 4–6

Eggs Bordelaise

½ gill claret
3 peeled shallots
1 tablespoon butter
1 dessertspoon flour
½ gill jellied stock
½ teaspoon minced chives
¼ teaspoon minced parsley
6 eggs
salt and pepper to taste
tarragon

Chop shallots. Melt butter in a small saucepan. Add shallots. Fry for 3 or 4 minutes, stirring frequently. Stir in flour. When frothy, stir in the claret and cook, stirring constantly until quantity is reduced by half. Add stock, chives, parsley, and a quarter teaspoon minced tarragon if available, otherwise a dash of tarragon powder. Stir till boiling. Cook gently for 10 minutes, stirring constantly. Break eggs into a shallow buttered fireproof dish. Season with salt and pepper to taste. Cover with the sauce. Bake in a moderate oven (350° F./Gas 4) for 6 minutes.

Serves 4–6

Marseillaise Eggs

1 tablespoon Madeira
1½ tablespoons foie gras
thick cream to taste
salt and pepper
pinch of ground mace
6 eggs
¼ teaspoon minced truffle

Remove any fat from foie gras. Rub the paste through a sieve into a basin. Gradually stir in enough cream to make the paste creamy. Season with salt and pepper to taste, and ground mace. Divide equally between 6 buttered ramekins. Break an egg into each ramekin. Season with salt and pepper. Place in a baking tin containing a little warm water. Bake in a moderate oven (350° F./Gas 4) for about 5 minutes. Meanwhile, boil the truffle in the Madeira for 5 minutes. When the eggs are ready, sprinkle a few drops of this mixture over each.

Serves 4–6

Lombardy Eggs

1 dessertspoon sherry
½ ounce butter
1 peeled shallot
1 ounce minced ham
1 dessertspoon flour
½ pint jellied stock
2 ounces mushrooms
6 hard-boiled eggs
1 dessertspoon grated Parmesan cheese

Melt butter in a saucepan. Mince shallots and add with ham. Cook, stirring constantly, over low heat, for 5 minutes, then stir in flour. When frothy, gradually stir in stock. Cook till boiling, stirring constantly, then slice mushrooms and add with the sherry. Boil for 5 minutes, still stirring, then pour over the eggs, shelled and arranged in a shallow buttered fireproof dish. Sprinkle with the cheese. Brown under the grill.

Serves 4–6

Swiss Scrambled Eggs

½ gill Chablis or Graves
8 ounces grated Swiss cheese
2 chopped shallots
1 teaspoon minced parsley
hot buttered toast as required
pinch of ground mace or grated nutmeg
black pepper
6 separated eggs

Place the cheese in the top of a double boiler. Add wine and shallots. Stir in parsley, ground mace or grated nutmeg and black pepper. Beat egg yolks. Add to mixture, then beat egg whites to a stiff froth. Stir the cheese mixture over hot water until the cheese melts, then beat the egg whites sharply and fold into the mixture in pan. Stir till scrambled. Turn gently into a shallow hot dish. Garnish with fingers of bread fried in butter, cutting the fingers from 2 slices of bread.

Serves 4–6

Mushroom Omelette

1 tablespoon sherry
½ ounce butter
4 ounces mushrooms
4 eggs
2 tablespoons milk or *rich stock*
salt and pepper to taste
pinch of crushed herbs

Peel, wash, dry and slice wild mushrooms, or slice the cultivated without peeling or washing. Melt butter in a small saucepan and add mushrooms. Fry for 5 minutes, stirring frequently. Add the sherry. Bring to the boil. Break eggs into a basin. Beat with the milk or stock for a moment or two. Season with salt, pepper and herbs. Melt enough butter in an omelette pan to cover the base. When it stops sizzling pour in the egg mixture. Fry omelette in the usual way. When almost ready, slide the mushrooms with any juice into the centre, then fold in two. Slide on to a flat hot dish and serve at once.

Serves 2–3

Fish

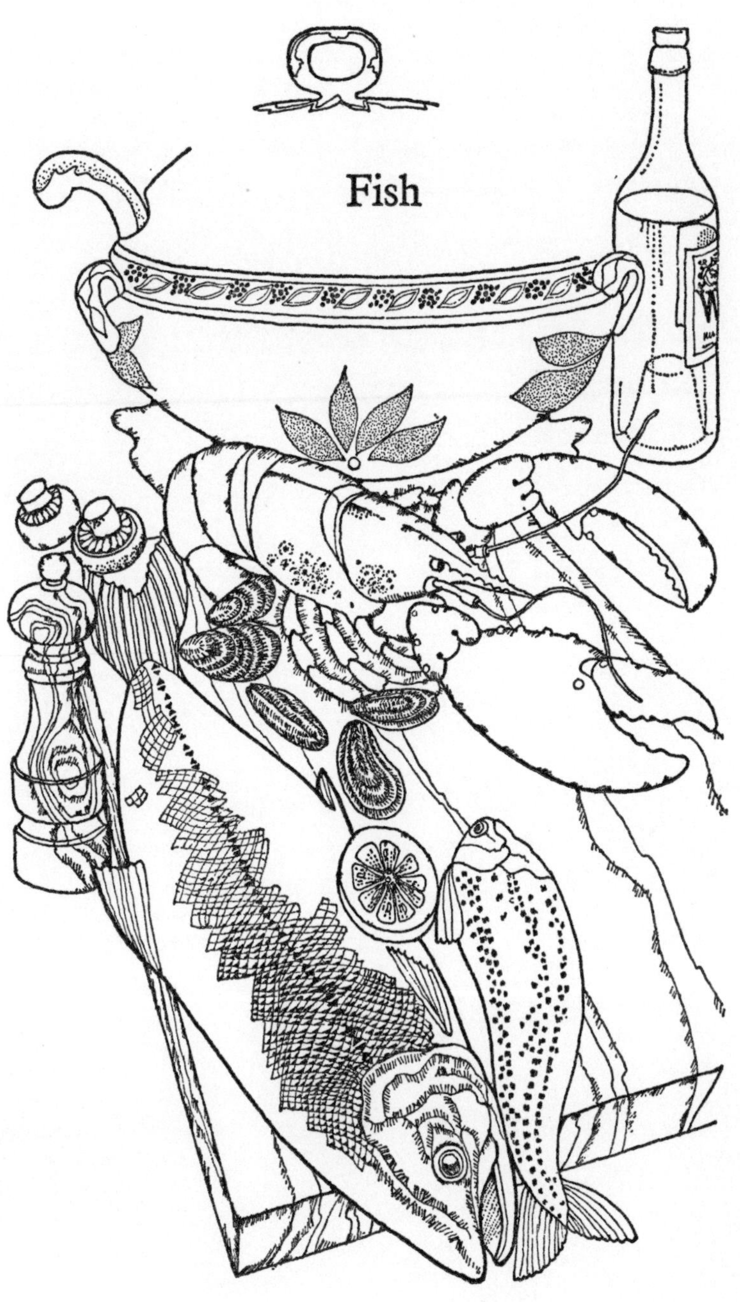

IN ADDITION to the following recipes for complete fish dishes, full instructions for the three main methods of cooking fish in liquid will be found in the Stocks, Sauces and Dressings section.

Baked Haddock

4 tablespoons white wine
4 pieces fresh haddock
tomato purée
1 clove garlic
parsley
breadcrumbs
salt and pepper
oil

Put a little oil in a round baking dish or tin. Put the haddock in it; cut into pieces of equal size. Pour the white wine over it, cover with the tomato purée; cover whole with white breadcrumbs, finely chopped garlic and parsley. Put into the oven (350°F./Gas 4) for 15 minutes.

Serves 4

Sole Bonne Femme

1½ gills white wine
a 2-pound sole (or 2 of 1 pound)
¾ pound mushrooms
6 tablespoons fish stock
5 ounces butter
1 teaspoon flour
1 ounce chopped shallot
1 teaspoon parsley
salt and pepper

Use a large oblong and shallow fireproof dish. Butter it generously, sprinkle with the parsley, shallot and mushrooms, and lay the fish on top, white side uppermost. Season with salt and pepper and add the fish stock and wine. (If no fish stock is available, use water.) Dot with 1 ounce butter divided into small pieces. Bring to the boil, then put in a moderate oven (350°F./Gas 4) and simmer gently for about 20 minutes, basting every 5–6 minutes. Remove the fish from the oven, tilt it, and carefully pour the liquid into a small thick saucepan. Rapidly reduce it to 1 gill, thickening it with the flour worked into ½ ounce butter. Remove the saucepan from the heat, add the remaining butter, divided into small pieces, and whisk rapidly. Meanwhile, the fish, mushrooms, etc. should have been kept warm in the oven. Pour the sauce over the fish just before serving.

Serves 4

Baked Stuffed Haddock Fillets

1 gill dry white wine
2 tablespoons dry French vermouth or *a similar Italian dry vermouth*
4 large haddock fillets
butter
1 egg
6 tablespoons chopped celery
2 tablespoons chopped parsley
salt and pepper
9 ounces breadcrumbs
4 ounces chopped spring onions
1 teaspoon marjoram
1 teaspoon tarragon

Brush the fillets with melted butter and season with salt and pepper. For the stuffing, mix together the breadcrumbs, onions, celery, marjoram, tarragon and parsley. Moisten with the dry vermouth and, if necessary, a little of the white wine, and bind with a well beaten egg. Put half of the fillets on a buttered baking dish. Spread them with the stuffing and then place on them the remaining fillets. Without any covering bake in a moderate oven until done, about 25 minutes, basting occasionally with the white wine.

Serves 4

Grilled Plaice with Wine Sauce

½ pint dry white wine
1 large filleted plaice
butter
lemon juice
salt and pepper
1 onion
1 tablespoon flour
3 teaspoons water
stuffed olives sliced

Place the fillets of plaice skin side down on a buttered shallow pan. Sprinkle with the lemon juice and salt and pepper. Spread the thinly sliced onion over the surface of the fish. Dot with butter and place under the grill. When the butter has melted, baste with the white wine. Basting frequently, grill until the fish easily separates when tested with a fork. Remove from pan and place on a hot serving dish. Thicken the liquor in the pan with one tablespoon flour and 3 teaspoons of warm water. Add to the sauce some sliced stuffed olives and pour over the fish.

Serves 4

Kedgeree

5 ounces sherry
2 pounds haddock fillets
2 tablespoons butter
3 cups cooked rice
2 hard-boiled eggs
salt and pepper
water
4 cloves
4 bay leaves
2 tablespoons chopped parsley
1 onion
4 teaspoons curry powder
1 teaspoon Worcestershire sauce

Cut the fish into pieces and cover with boiling water into which has been added 3 ounces of the sherry, salt and pepper, the cloves and bay leaves. Simmer for about 20 minutes, or until tender. In another saucepan melt the two tablespoons butter and fry the onion, chopped fine, until tender. Add 3 cups cooked rice, 2 chopped hard-boiled eggs, the chopped parsley; sprinkle in 4 teaspoons of curry powder and one teaspoon Worcestershire sauce. Next remove bones from the fish, if any, flake, and put into the rice mixture. Now moisten with the sherry, stir well, and place in a covered casserole. Bake in the oven for ten minutes at (400°F./Gas 6). Before serving, garnish with slices of hard-boiled eggs.

Serves 4

Tuna Fish with Sherry

2 tablespoons sherry
1 can tuna fish
1 packet potato crisps
1 can condensed cream of mushroom soup

Cover the bottom of an ovenproof baking dish with potato crisps. Then cover with a layer of broken up tuna fish. Top with another layer of potato crisps. Next, pour a little of the cream of mushroom soup over the contents of the dish. Stir two tablespoons of sherry into what remains of the soup and pour it all over the tuna and potato crisps. Bake in a moderate oven for 20–30 minutes.

Serves 4

Fillets of Sole in White Wine

½ pint dry white wine
4 large fillets of sole
3–4 mushrooms
1 tablespoon butter
½ pint consommé
1 teaspoon chopped onion
1 stalk celery
2 tablespoons cream
salt and pepper
grated Parmesan cheese
1 bay leaf
1 teaspoon chopped parsley

Sprinkle the fillets of sole with salt and pepper. Melt the butter in a large frying pan and add the chopped onion, parsley, mushrooms (chopped fine), one stalk celery, bay leaf, the white wine and the consommé. Place the fillets in the hot liquid and simmer for 5 to 10 minutes, or until barely tender. Then carefully remove to a shallow baking dish. Boil the liquor in which the sole was cooked until reduced to about a little less than half a pint. Add the cream, and additional seasoning if necessary. Strain the liquor over the fish in the baking dish. Sprinkle the grated cheese over all and bake on the upper shelf of a hot oven for about ten minutes when the top should be lightly browned.

Serves 4

Halibut in Curry Sauce

½ pint dry white wine
2 pounds halibut
4 ounces butter
1 cup fine breadcrumbs
3 tablespoons flour
½ green pepper
1 teaspoon lemon juice
1 small onion
1 celery stalk
1 teaspoon curry powder
salt and pepper

Put the wine in a dish or bowl and dip the halibut steaks in it; then dip the breadcrumbs in it, seasoned with salt and pepper. Heat 2 ounces of the butter in a fireproof dish; place the halibut steaks in this, baste with the hot butter and bake uncovered for about 10 minutes, i.e. until the crumbs are brown and the fish easily flakes with a fork. In a saucepan melt 2 ounces butter, add the onion, peeled and chopped finely, half a green pepper and the chopped celery. Sauté for 10 minutes over low heat. Mix the curry powder with the flour, stirring thoroughly, and add the remaining white wine. Stir well and add the lemon juice. Bring to the boil, stirring. Pour the hot sauce over the halibut.

Serves 4

Braised Halibut

½ pint dry white wine
1½–2 pounds halibut
flour
salt and pepper
butter
4 tablespoons water
parsley
tarragon
chives
3 ounces white mushrooms
lemon juice
arrowroot
Half a 5-ounce carton of double cream

Choose an oval or oblong oven into which the halibut will fit neatly. Pass the fish through seasoned flour and shake off any excess. Place in the buttered dish and sprinkle over it the white wine, the water and the parsley, tarragon and chives. Cover with a lid or foil and bake for up to 30 minutes. After removing the dark skin, divide the fish into 4 pieces at their 'natural' markings and place them on a heated dish. Slice the mushrooms and cook them in a little butter, a tablespoon of water and a squeeze of lemon juice in a covered pan for a minute. Strain both the fish and mushroom stock into a small pan and boil to reduce them to about 4 tablespoons. Add the mushrooms and half a level teaspoon of arrowroot blended with the cream, and bring to the boil. Add ½ ounce butter and turn the pan this way and that to blend it into the sauce. Pour this over the fish. Serve creamy mashed potatoes with the fish.

Serves 4

Sole with French Vermouth

3½ tablespoons dry French vermouth
1 glass dry white wine
1 larged filleted sole
butter
flour
lemon juice

Poach the sole in some fish stock to which has been added the measure of dry vermouth. Remove the fish, place on a serving dish and keep hot. Thicken the sauce with walnut sized knobs of butter rolled in flour, add a glass of dry white wine and a squeeze of lemon. Pour over the fish and serve hot.

Serves 2

Salmon Parisienne

½ bottle white wine
1 salmon (about 2 pounds)
3 eggs
1 lettuce
carrots
1 onion
salt and pepper
bouquet garni

Choose a salmon with a short round body, bright eyes and red gills. Clean through the gills and wash. Fix on to the grill of a fish kettle and fill the kettle with a highly spiced court-bouillon made from the sliced carrots and onion, bouquet garni and ⅔ water to ⅓ dry white wine. Bring to the boil and simmer for about one hour. Take out the salmon, drain and remove the skin. Place on a bed of lettuce leaves. Decorate the salmon with flowers made from tomato skin and tarragon leaves. Cut the eggs, having boiled them hard, into halves and place round the salmon. Serve mayonnaise in small puffed pastry cases. A sheet of gelatine can be melted in a little strained court-bouillon and poured over the decorated salmon, when cool, before putting in the refrigerator.

Serves 4–5

Hake in White Wine Sauce

2 tablespoons white wine
6 thick slices of hake
1 onion (sliced)
3 tomatoes
1 tablespoon olive oil
a little flour
1 lemon

Fry the hake in the oil with the sliced onion until golden brown. Remove and replace with the tomatoes (the seeds having been removed) diced or sieved. Thicken with a little flour and make thinner with the white wine. Put the fish back to cook for about 20 minutes without bringing it to the boil. Place on a hot dish. Strain the sauce and pour over the hake, adding the juice of a lemon.

Serves 6

Sole with Black and Green Grapes

¼ pint white wine
4 large fillets sole
2 ounces mushrooms
lemon juice
chopped parsley
¼ pound black grapes
¼ pound green grapes
1 egg yolk
¼ pint cream
butter
salt and pepper

Skin the fillets and roll up tightly. Skin the grapes, cut in half and remove the pips. Peel the mushrooms and slice them very thinly. Melt a small knob of butter in a heavy saucepan, add the wine, the grapes and the mushrooms. Place the fillets on top and season each with salt and pepper and a squeeze of lemon juice. Cook gently for about 15 minutes and when cooked lift the fillets on to a hot dish and place alternately with small piles of grapes. Allow the liquid to reduce to less than half by boiling quickly in the open pan. Remove from the heat, allow to cool slightly, add the cream and beat in the egg yolk. Add more seasoning and lemon juice if necessary. Reheat without boiling. Coat each fillet with the sauce and sprinkle with chopped parsley.

Serves 4

Fillets of Brill

½ gill Madeira, sherry or *white wine*
4 medium tomatoes
3 ounces rice
3 ounces butter
1 ounce Parmesan cheese
paprika
lemon juice
4 large fillets of brill
2½ gills tomato sauce
some chopped cooked ham
1 small onion
1 pint fish stock
salt and pepper

Melt the butter in a saucepan and add the peeled and chopped onion. Fry, stirring occasionally till clear. Meanwhile butter a fireproof dish and place in folded fillets side by side. Sprinkle them with salt, pepper and paprika to taste. Add lemon juice and wine. Cover with buttered paper. Bake in a moderate oven (300°F./Gas 2) for 10 minutes. When rice has fried for 5–6 minutes, stir in stock and cook till absorbed and rice is soft, then add ½ gill tomato sauce and season to taste. Cook for a moment or two longer, then stir in the cheese and chopped ham. Halve the tomatoes. Remove centres. Fill with the hot risotto. Bake in the oven for 5 minutes. Serve fillets in the centre of a hot dish with stuffed halves of tomato round. Strain the liquor from the fish into the remainder of the tomato sauce and serve in a hot sauce boat. Garnish with fresh parsley.

Serves 4

Baked Red Mullet

3½ tablespoons claret
2 ounces melted butter
6 medium red mullet
2 teaspoons lemon juice
1 teaspoon anchovy essence
cayenne

Clean, wash and dry the fish carefully, retaining the liver. Wrap each fish closely in a sheet of buttered foil and close ends tightly. Place in a greased baking dish side by side. Bake in a moderate oven (300°F./Gas 2) for 30 minutes, then carefully remove paper and arrange on a hot dish. Drain liquor out of foil into a saucepan. Stir in melted butter, anchovy essence, claret, lemon juice, and cayenne to taste. Pour over fish. Serve at once.

Serves 6

Baked Trout

1 pint dry white wine
4 fresh trout
1 onion
1 shallot
2 cloves garlic
1 leaf tarragon
parsley
2 tablespoons olive oil
5 tablespoons water
1 teaspoon butter
2 tablespoons fresh cream
2 egg yolks
lemon juice
salt and pepper

Clean the trout without removing the scales. Leave to soak in fresh water for 10 minutes. Drain well and arrange in a baking dish. Chop the onion, shallot, garlic, tarragon and parsley small and sauté them for 10 minutes in the olive oil. Add the wine and the water. Season with salt and pepper. Continue cooking over medium heat for 10 more minutes. Pour over the trout, cover, and simmer for 20 minutes in a moderate oven (300°F./Gas 2).

Remove the trout and keep them hot. Thicken the liquid with the butter, cream and egg yolks together with a little lemon juice. Pour the sauce over the trout in the serving dish.

Serves 4

Scallops

½ pint dry white wine
8 or 9 scallops
1 chopped onion
bouquet garni
½ small clove garlic
salt and pepper
4 ounces fresh breadcrumbs
½ pound butter
1 dessertspoon chopped parsley
dry breadcrumbs

Remove the scallops from their shells and discard the black parts. Place the meat and coral in one basin and the beards in another. Wash all in several changes of water. Squeeze all the water from the beards and chop them finely. Meanwhile fry the onion slowly in 2 ounces butter. Mix the chopped beards with the fried onion. Add the bouquet garni and the garlic. Season with salt and pepper and simmer for 15 minutes. Slice the scallops thinly and poach in the white wine, and add to the simmering onion and beards. Continue cooking together slowly for an additional 15 minutes. Remove from the heat, add the fresh breadcrumbs, 3 ounces butter and the parsley. Butter the empty shells; fill ¾ full with the cooked scallops and onion. Arrange a strip of coral on each and sprinkle sparsely with the dry breadcrumbs. Divide the remaining butter into pieces and place one on the contents of each shell. Brown in the oven for 5 minutes. Serve hot.

Serves 4

Whiting au Gratin

3½ tablespoons white wine
6 medium sized whiting
shallots
2 ounces butter
2 ounces grated cheese
3 tablespoons cream
1 lemon

Put the fish in a buttered dish with the chopped shallots. Wet with white wine and cook in the oven at 300°F./Gas 2, basting often. Place the whiting in a second dish and cover with the reduced sauce sieved and thickened with the cream. Sprinkle with cheese and put in the oven. Add the juice of a lemon.

Serves 3

Trout Monaco

1 gill dry French vermouth or similar Italian vermouth
6 medium-sized trout
3½ tablespoons butter
2 egg yolks
1 gill cream
4 ounces grated Gruyère cheese
salt and pepper

Clean the trout, leaving the heads on. Wash them in fresh water, wipe with a cloth and arrange in a shallow fireproof dish. Season with salt and pepper, add the butter and white wine and heat through in the oven (at 300°F./Gas 2) with the door open. As soon as the trout are really hot, prepare a sauce with the egg yolks, cream, and the cooking liquor from the fish. Pour the sauce over the trout and then cover completely with the grated cheese. Bake in a very hot oven until golden brown, and serve.

Serves 6

Whiting Bercy

1 gill dry white wine
2 whiting about ¾ pound each
3½ tablespoons butter
2 chopped shallots
1 teaspoon chopped parsley
12 mushrooms (chopped)
1 bay leaf
salt and pepper

Wash and clean the whiting. Place a small nut of butter, a little chopped shallot and parsley on each fish. Grease an ovenproof dish generously with butter and sprinkle the bottom with a layer of chopped shallots and parsley. Then arrange the fish on it. Season with salt and pepper and pour the wine over the fish, the mushrooms previously sautéed in butter, a few small nuts of butter and the bay leaf. Cook first over a fairly brisk heat for 5 minutes, then bake in a hot oven for 20 minutes, basting frequently. Serve in the baking dish.

Serves 4

Red Mullet in White Wine

2½ gills dry white wine
2½–3 pounds red mullet
8 tablespoons tomato pulp or *1 small can drained tomatoes*
parsley
thyme
bay leaf
saffron (if desired)
1 lemon
salt and pepper

Have the fish cleaned and the heads removed, and arrange in a buttered fireproof dish. Cover with the wine and add the salt and pepper, tomato pulp, parsley, thyme, bay leaf, and saffron. Bring to the boil, reduce to low heat, and continue cooking for 10 minutes. Serve in the cooking liquor with a slice of peeled lemon on each portion of fish. This dish is usually served cold, but may be served hot if preferred.

Serves 4

Salmon Trout in Rosé Wine

1¼ pints rosé wine
1 salmon trout (4–5 pounds)
bouquet garni
2 tablespoons gelatin
slices of lemon
croûtons
½ pint mayonnaise
salt and pepper

Clean the fish, leaving on the head. Poach in a court-bouillon made with the rosé wine, salt, pepper, and the bouquet garni. Remove the fish when done. Reduce the court-bouillon to half. Soak the gelatin in a little water, add to the court-bouillon, and allow to cool. Remove the skin from one side of the fish only and arrange it on a long platter. Glaze with the court-bouillon and decorate with the lemon slices and croûtons.

Serve cold, with mayonnaise.

Serves 6–8

Trout Espagnole

3½ tablespoons white wine
a few small trout
4–5 shallots
4–5 small mushrooms
chopped parsley
1 tablespoon chopped chives
1–2 tablespoons honey
oil
a sprinkling of cumin
salt and pepper

Put the fish in a casserole with the oil, the wine, the honey and the chopped shallots, and season with cumin, salt and pepper. Allow the fish to stand in this marinade for about an hour, then take them out, wrap each fish in foil, well oiled. Put them in an earthenware casserole and cook on very low heat until tender. When ready, remove from the foil, put on a hot dish and serve with a butter sauce.

Serves 4

Poached Turbot

1 glass white wine
4 fillets turbot
1 glass fish stock
2 ounces butter
1 tablespoon flour
pepper and salt
juice of ½ lemon
parsley

Poach the fillets in the wine and stock in a medium oven for 15 minutes. Place on a dish and keep warm. Melt 1 ounce butter and add the flour. Mix well and strain the liquor from the poached fillets into the pan. Stir well and simmer gently for 10 minutes. Mix in the lemon juice and stir in the remaining ounce of butter.

Pepper and salt to taste. Glaze the fish with the sauce and garnish with parsley.

Serves 4

Crawfish in White Wine Sauce

1½ pints dry white wine
24 crawfish
4 sliced onions
salt and peppercorns
2 sliced carrots
10 shallots
bouquet garni of parsley, thyme and chervil

Prepare a court-bouillon with the white wine, onions, carrots, shallots and bouquet garni. Add some salt and a few peppercorns. Bring the court-bouillon to the boil and allow to simmer until the liquid is reduced to one half of the original amount. Wash and drain crawfish carefully. Boil them in the court-bouillon for 10 to 12 minutes. Remove the crawfish. Arrange in a soup tureen and pour the court-bouillon over them through a strainer.

Serves 4–6

Mussels in Sauce

¼ pint dry white wine
2 quarts fresh mussels
4 shallots
1 tablespoon butter
1 tablespoon flour
parsley
milk
4 tablespoons breadcrumbs
1 tablespoon tomato sauce
salt and pepper

Wash the mussels in cold water and scrub carefully, removing any foreign matter. Put them into a deep saucepan, add the white wine and a pinch of pepper. Cover. Sauté, shaking the pan from time to time, until the mussels are well open (6 to 8 minutes). Discard the extra shells, retaining only those with mussels attached. Strain through a very fine strainer to retain any sand. Put the mussels aside and conserve the broth. Prepare a roux by mixing together the butter and the flour in a saucepan. Let it cool until lukewarm, and mix with half of the broth. Mince the shallots and add an equal quantity of parsley also minced. Then add the breadcrumbs moistened with milk. Add the other part of the broth and also the tomato sauce. Season to taste with salt and pepper. If the sauce is too thick, thin it with dry white wine and an equal quantity of water. Put the mussels in the sauce in the covered saucepan and simmer for 10 minutes. Serve in soup plates and add broth.

Serves 4

Herring Salad

1 wine glass of claret
10 salt herrings
cooked veal
potatoes
beetroot
apples
2 small pickled gherkins
4 tablespoons vinegar
4 tablespoons oil
a little sugar
hard-boiled egg

Soak the herrings in cold water for 5–6 hours. Remove from the water and dry the fish. Take the same weight of cooked veal, the same of potatoes, beetroot and apples and 2 small pickled cucumbers. Cut all the ingredients in small cubes and place in the salad bowl. Mix 2 tablespoons vinegar with 2 of oil, a little sugar, 1 wine glass of claret, and the juice from the beetroot. Pour this dressing over the salad and allow to stand for 12 hours. Before serving cover with a sauce made from 2 tablespoons oil and 2 of vinegar, seasoned with salt and pepper. Put the oil and vinegar in a small saucepan and stand this in a larger one, in boiling water. Stir the oil and vinegar until the mixture becomes quite thick. Garnish the salad with hard-boiled egg and beetroot.

Serves 4–6

Meat

MANY OF the dishes in this section may be served as a complete course, with no other accompaniment than plain boiled, chipped or straw potatoes, rice or pasta.

Many, too, are ideal for entertaining because they can be prepared in advance; some can be reheated when you need them and, because of the long cooking time, also keep better than many other meat dishes. Not only this, but because all the work has been done at the initial stages of preparation, the hostess has plenty of time to receive her guests at leisure without having to disappear for a long session in the kitchen.

Note: all cuts of meat have the same nutritive value (including animal proteins, fats, mineral salts and vitamins) whether or not they are cooked in wine. Grilled and boiled meat both create a similar nutritive balance in the organism, but the individual's ability to digest them may of course vary.

Loin of Pork with Prunes

1 gill dry white wine
4 loin of pork chops
25 prunes
flour
butter
⅓ tablespoon redcurrant jelly
½ pint cream
salt and pepper

Soak the prunes in the wine for 24 hours. Remove the stones. Flour and fry the chops to a golden brown in very hot butter, seasoning with salt and pepper while cooking. Then remove the chops and arrange on a long dish. Keep warm. Meanwhile, boil the prunes for half an hour in the wine. Arrange on the dish round the pork chops. Pour the cooking liquor from the prunes into a saucepan and reduce a little. Add the redcurrant jelly and bind with the cream. Pour over the pork and serve very hot.

Serves 4

Veal Stew

5 tablespoons red wine
2 pounds breast of veal
1½ tablespoons flour
2½ tablespoons butter
12 small onions
4 diced carrots
bouquet garni
fried croûtons

Cut the veal into pieces and blanch in boiling water. In a deep skillet prepare a roux (by mixing the flour and butter to a smooth paste); add the red wine, onions, carrots and bouquet garni. Add the veal and simmer for 1½ hours. Reduce the cooking liquor slightly. Serve with fried croûtons.

Serves 4–5

Chererie

1 tablespoon sherry
some cold (cooked) meat
1 saltspoon salt
½ saltspoon cayenne
1 tablespoon chopped onion
1 tablespoon vinegar
1 tablespoon ketchup
1 tablespoon redcurrant jelly
½ pint stock
flour

Cut the meat into thin slices put into a saucepan with the rest of the ingredients, until thoroughly hot. Remove the meat and thicken the gravy with flour.

Serves 4

Liver with Mushrooms

4 tablespoons medium sherry
1 pound sliced calf's liver
flour
2 ounces butter
1 teaspoon Worcestershire sauce
salt and pepper
1 10½-ounce can condensed beef consommé
2 tablespoons grated onion
¼ pound cooked sliced mushrooms
generous pinch of thyme
2 tablespoons chopped parsley

Cut off any skin on the liver and cut up slices into strips. Roll in flour. Melt 1½ tablespoons of the butter in a large frying pan. Add the liver and onion, sauté quickly until the liver is just brown, stirring frequently. Remove the liver from the pan and blend in 3 tablespoons flour. Add the consommé and the liquid from the mushrooms and cook, stirring until the mixture is thick and smooth. Add the wine, Worcestershire sauce, thyme, mushrooms, parsley, and salt and pepper to taste. Put the liver into the sauce and heat until it is piping hot.
Note: Remember that cooking too long makes liver become tough.

Serves 4

Sausages in Wine

½ pint white wine
1 pound small sausages
3 tablespoons breadcrumbs
watercress (chopped)

Partially fry some small sausages until not quite cooked through. Drain off the fat. Add to the fat the breadcrumbs and fry to a light brown. Remove from the heat and stir in ½ pint white wine and stir together until they boil. Add the sausages and simmer for 10 minutes. Garnish generously with chopped watercress.

Serves 3

Braised Veal Chops

5 tablespoons dry sherry
4 thick veal chops
1½ ounces butter
½ pint beef stock
a good pinch each of marjoram and sweet basil
¼ pound sliced fried mushrooms
3 tablespoons flour
1 tablespoon tomato purée
garlic salt
salt and pepper

Heat the butter in a large heavy metal casserole and brown chops slowly on each side. Remove the chops from the casserole. Add flour to the remaining fat and blend well. Add the beef stock and the wine. Cook until the mixture boils and thickens. Blend in the tomato purée, and add the mushrooms and seasonings. Place the chops in the sauce. Cover and bake in a moderate oven (350°F./Gas 4) for 1 hour, or until the chops are tender, turning and basting them several times.

Serves 4

Braised Shoulder of Lamb

½ pint dry red wine
3 tablespoons medium sherry
shoulder of lamb (boned and rolled)
flour
salt and pepper
3–4 peppercorns
pinch of thyme
2 tablespoons chopped parsley
½ pint boiling water
1 ounce butter
1 large chopped onion
1 clove garlic
1 bay leaf
2 teaspoons rosemary

Dredge lamb with flour seasoned with salt and pepper. Heat butter in a heavy saucepan and brown lamb slowly on all sides. Add the wine, water, onion, crushed garlic, bay leaf, thyme, peppercorns, rosemary and salt to taste. Cover tightly and simmer gently for 2–2½ hours, or until the meat is tender, turning occasionally.

Serves 6

Braised Pork Chops

5 tablespoons medium sherry
4 pork chops about 1¼ inches thick
¼ pint sour cream
¼ teaspoon paprika
4 tablespoons cooked or canned tomatoes
flour
½ teaspoon Worcestershire sauce
salt and pepper

Toss the pork chops in flour seasoned with salt and pepper. Brown slowly on each side in a large heavy frying pan, using any fat cut from the chops. Then pour off any superfluous fat. Mix the remaining ingredients, add salt and pepper and pour over the chops. Cover and simmer gently until the chops are tender (about an hour), turning and basting occasionally.

Serves 4

Calf's Liver Sautéed with Red Wine

1 gill red wine
1½ pounds calf's liver
salt and pepper
thyme
seasoned flour
2 onions
butter
bay leaf

Toss the sliced liver in seasoned flour and sprinkle with the crushed bay leaf and thyme. Melt some butter in a heavy frying pan, and brown the sliced onions until soft. Remove the onions and fry the liver over a high heat in the pan, adding more butter if necessary. Put the cooked onions back in the pan with the liver and add the red wine. Leave over high heat for a couple of minutes and serve at once.

Serves 3–4

Rump Steak with Wine Sauce

1 gill dry white wine
2 large rump steaks
6 shallots
salt and pepper
1 tablespoon butter
1 level dessertspoon Dijon mustard

Chop the shallots fine and fry lightly in butter. Mix the mustard with the white wine and add to the shallots. Reduce slightly over a low heat. Sear the meat on both sides. Season with salt and pepper. Pour sauce over the steaks and serve hot.

Serves 2

Beef Kidney in Red Wine

1 pint dry red wine
1 beef kidney
1 onion
1½ ounces butter
½ clove garlic
salt and pepper
1 tablespoon flour
good pinch of tarragon
1 medium-sized (about 13/14 ounces) can tomatoes

Remove the skin and centre from the kidney and cut into slices or pieces. Sauté the kidney with the sliced onion, crushed garlic and salt and pepper in 1 ounce melted butter for about 5 minutes, or until cooked. Then remove the kidney. Add the flour to what remains in the pan and stir thoroughly. Add the tomatoes and season to taste, then pour in the red wine. Allow to simmer for about 10 minutes. Meanwhile melt 1 tablespoon butter in another saucepan and allow to become brown; add the kidney. Then add both kidney and liquor to the onion and tomatoes and

Pork Spareribs Hawaii (*page* 67)

Rabbit in White Wine (*page* 89)

allow to cook without a cover until the gravy is as thick as desired. Transfer to a hot dish.

Serves 4

Beef in Burgundy

½ pint Burgundy
3 pounds spareribs of beef
salt and pepper
3 tablespoons Worcestershire sauce
3 apples
2 chopped onions
3 tablespoons brown sugar

Sprinkle the beef with salt and pepper and place in a roasting pan. Cover with the onion. Place the peeled apples, cored and cut in half, around the meat. Mix the Worcestershire sauce with half of the Burgundy and trickle it over the beef and apples. Now sprinkle the brown sugar over the apples. Cover and roast in a hot oven (375°F./Gas 5) for 1 hour. Uncover and pour over it the remainder of the Burgundy and continue roasting until brown (about ¼ hour), occasionally basting. Remove to a hot dish.

Serves 4

Braised Oxtail

red wine
1 large oxtail
bouillon
1 can tomatoes
1 cup sliced mushrooms
3 tablespoons cooking fat
1 tablespoon chopped onion
5 ounces chopped celery
5 ounces chopped carrots
seasoned flour
1 crushed clove garlic
salt and pepper

Note: This dish is improved if made the day before required.
Have the oxtail chopped into pieces. Wash and then cover with boiling water for a few minutes. Pour away the water and dry the oxtail. Dredge with seasoned flour. Heat the fat in a heavy saucepan and add the oxtail, carrots, onion, celery, tomatoes

and garlic. Cook over a high heat until lightly browned, stirring constantly.

Now transfer into an iron casserole and add enough red wine and bouillon in equal quantities to cover the ingredients. Bring to the boil then cover and place in a moderate oven (350°F./Gas 4) and let it cook for 2 hours. Allow to stand overnight and the next day skim off the fat. Add the sliced mushrooms to the contents of the pan, bring to the boil, and cook gently for about half an hour. Transfer to a hot dish.

Serves 4

Steak as in Burgundy

½ pint dry red wine
1½–2 pounds steak
6 tablespoons butter
1 tablespoon chopped parsley
1 small onion
salt
black pepper

Fry the onion, chopped very fine, in a small saucepan in half of the butter for about 4 minutes. Add the parsley and red wine and allow it to simmer gently while the steak is being fried in a heavy frying pan. When the steak is done to your taste, remove it to a hot dish and add the remainder of the butter to the liquor from the steak. Add the onion and the wine to the pan when the butter has melted and stir thoroughly. Add the salt and pepper, allow it to come to the boil, then pour over the steak.

Serves 2–3

Veal with Wine and Orange Sauce

7 tablespoons dry white wine
2½ pounds roasting veal
2 pounds carrots
4 medium onions
6 oranges
1 thick rasher of fat bacon
butter
oil
salt and pepper

Heat 2 ounces butter and one tablespoon oil in a thick saucepan and seal the meat on all sides surrounded by the onions cut in half. Add salt and pepper to taste, together with two carrots finely sliced, and one glass white wine. Cover and cook gently for 1 hour. Then add the juice of 4 oranges and simmer for a further 15 minutes. In the meantime, cut the bacon into thin strips and fry them in another saucepan in one ounce butter. Add the rest of the carrots thinly sliced and seasoned to taste, and moistened, but not quite covered, with some of the liquor from the meat pan. Place the meat on a large dish and surround it with the carrot slices and two more oranges cut into flat rounds. Pour a second glass of white wine into the meat saucepan, stir well into the remaining juices, and reduce on a low flame until the newly added wine loses its acidity but still retains its flavour to the sauce. Pour over meat and carrots.

Serves 6

Roast Lamb as in Rome

white wine
leg of lamb
rosemary
marjoram
clove of garlic
salt and pepper
juice of ½ lemon
celery, carrots and turnips

Insert a clove of garlic and a sprig of rosemary between the bone and the flesh of the lamb and add pepper and salt. Sprinkle with white wine and cook at 375°/400°F (Gas 5/6). Lower the temperature every 10 minutes, and baste the joint with white wine. For the last 20 minutes of cooking surround the meat with chopped celery including the tops, carrots and turnips. When the lamb is cooked, squeeze the juice of half a lemon over it and sprinkle it with chopped marjoram.

Serves 6–8

Ham Baked in Port

1½ gills port
1 thick slice ham
3 ounces brown sugar
3 generous tablespoons prepared mustard

Rub the brown sugar into both sides of the ham and follow this by rubbing in the mustard. Put the ham in a baking dish and add the port. Bake in a moderate oven for about one hour, basting occasionally with the port. Remove the ham to a hot dish. Skim the fat off the liquor and pour in a little more port if necessary. Stir well and pour over the ham.

Serves 4

Devilled Hamburgers

4 tablespoons red wine
1 pound minced chuck steak
4 ounces breadcrumbs
3 tablespoons chilli sauce
1 minced clove garlic
1 teaspoon Worcestershire sauce
salt and pepper
1 teaspoon made mustard
1 tablespoon minced onion
½ teaspoon mace
1 teaspoon horseradish

Mix well together the steak, Worcestershire sauce, chilli sauce, onion, mustard, horseradish, breadcrumbs, salt and black pepper to taste, the red wine, garlic and mace. Make into flat cakes and grill for 3–4 minutes on each side, according to how well done you like them.

Serves 4

Pork Chops in Madeira

3½ tablespoons Madeira
4 loin of pork chops
3 tablespoons sour cream
salt and pepper

Fry the pork chops. When nicely browned and tender, remove them from the pan. If there is too much fat in the pan, pour it off. Add the Madeira and the sour cream and mix well into the gravy. Replace the pork chops and cook, basting frequently, for another 5–10 minutes, according to the thickness of the chops.

Serves 4

Loin of Pork and Exotic Sauce

1 glass white wine
a loin of pork (7–8 chops)
1 large clove of garlic
salt and pepper
thyme
coriander seeds
1 tablespoon brown sugar
1 tablespoon breadcrumbs
1 tablespoon chopped parsley
1 teaspoon dry mustard
watercress

Get your butcher to chine the loin but do not remove the bone until after the joint is cooked. The rind should also be removed so that there is not more than half an inch of fat left. But retain the rind and cook the meat on it, for it improves the sauce.

With your sharpest knife, make little slits in the flesh of the meat; place a little sliver of garlic in each (use one clove only, or it will spoil the other flavours). Then rub the surface of the meat with salt and shake a dusting of powdered thyme on it. Next, take a generous handful of coriander seeds and dot them about in as many crevasses as you can find. Now tip a glass of white wine over the whole thing and leave it to marinate for as long as possible: ½ an hour will do but 2–3 hours is better. Now set it, fat uppermost, in a baking tin with all the marinade to keep it moist (the marinade will turn into delicious sauce). Cover the top with a piece of foil so that the top becomes tacky. Meanwhile start it off at 350°F./Gas 4, and leave for about an hour, looking at it half way through to make sure the marinade has not dried up. If it has, add more wine (or water). Take 1 tablespoon of brown sugar, the same of breadcrumbs and chopped parsley, and a teaspoon of dry mustard: mix them together for the topping After the first hour, take the pork from the oven and remove the foil. Then gently press the mixture into the fat with the back of a spoon or a palette knife, and put back into the oven for another 40 minutes. Baste with the marinade from time to time so that the crust turns a nice shade of brown. Test it with a knife to see if it feels done. Carefully place the loin on a bed of watercress. Throw away the piece of rind, quickly heat the marinade and serve it separately as sauce.

Serves 6–8

Filet Mignon with Béarnaise Sauce

2 tablespoons white wine
4 fillet steaks
butter
2 tablespoons tarragon vinegar
½ teaspoon chopped shallot
tarragon
cayenne
salt and pepper
2 egg yolks
chervil

Brush the fillets with a little melted butter. Place them close to the grill at high heat and grill them for about 3 minutes on each side a little less if preferred rare, or a little longer if preferred well done. Season them with salt and pepper.

For the Béarnaise sauce: place in a small pan two tablespoons each of white wine and tarragon vinegar, half a teaspoon chopped shallot, a tiny pinch of tarragon, a few grains of cayenne, a small nut of butter, salt and freshly milled pepper to taste. Bring to the boil and simmer to reduce by two-thirds. Remove from the heat and stir in two egg yolks. Place over a low heat and, stirring all the time, gradually add 4 ounces softened butter, a little at a time. Never let the sauce become too warm because it could then separate. When nicely thickened rub through a nylon sieve and add a little finely chopped tarragon and chervil. Serve this sauce with the steaks.

Serves 4

Braised Knuckle of Veal

2 tablespoons dry French vermouth or *similar dry Italian vermouth*
1 large knuckle of veal
1½ tablespoons flour
3 ounces butter
½ pound small mushrooms
celery salt and black pepper
2 tablespoons cooking oil
bouquet garni
½ teaspoon paprika
a little grated orange peel

Fry the knuckle slowly in butter and oil, until golden brown. Sprinkle in the flour and brown. Add the dry vermouth, the bouquet garni, salt and pepper and hot water to cover.

Place the lid on pan and cook gently for one hour. Add the paprika and a little grated orange rind blended with a little of the stock. Cover and cook for ¾ hour. Cook the mushrooms in a little butter and add to the veal. Remove the bouquet garni before serving.

Serves 4

Ham in Tarragon Sauce

¼ pint dry white wine
½ pound canned or boiled ham
tarragon
½ ounce flour
½ ounce butter
½ pint chicken stock

Boil together the chicken stock and the white wine. Add a slightly bruised sprig of tarragon, then gently simmer to reduce the stock to ½ pint. Simmer ½ ounce flour in ½ ounce butter without colouring it. Away from the heat add the strained stock. Return to the heat and stir while it is coming to the boil. Add 4–6 finely chopped tarragon leaves and ½ pound canned or boiled ham cut in fairly thick slices. Warm through, then serve with plainly boiled spinach or sprouts and boiled small potatoes turned in butter.

Serves 2–3

Pork Chops with a Difference

1 glass green ginger wine
4 pork chops
2 ounces butter
3 cooking apples
salt and pepper
cinnamon

Season the chops with salt and pepper and brown them in butter in a casserole. Peel, core and slice the apples and toss them in the butter without browning them. Add a pinch of cinnamon.

Place the chops on the apple and sprinkle on the ginger wine. Put in a small piece of butter on each chop. Place the lid on the casserole and cook in a moderate oven for ½ hour.

Serves 4

Entrecôte with White Wine

3 gills white wine
about 2 pounds steak (cut from between the ribs)
4½ ounces shallots
2 ounces butter
salt and pepper
parsley
half a lemon

Chop the shallots and cook them in the white wine. When it is completely reduced take away from the heat. Add the butter and, when melted, the juice of half a lemon and the chopped parsley. Pour this sauce over the grilled steak. Before grilling the steak smear it with oil.

Serves 3

Fillets of Veal in Port

½ pint port
6 fillets of veal
butter
1 beaten egg
12 ounces stale breadcrumbs
salt and pepper

Sprinkle fillets with salt and pepper to taste, then soak them in the port for 1 hour. If large, use more port as the fillets must be entirely covered. When required, dip in beaten egg, then bread-crumbs, and fry in smoking hot butter. Serve with the port as a gravy, heated and poured into a hot sauceboat.

Serves 6

Goulash

¼ pint red wine
1 pound stewing beef
1 large potato
2 large onions
bouquet garni
juice of ½ lemon
seasoned flour
clove of garlic
2 ounces fat
½ pint good stock
2 ounces bacon
¼ teaspoon paprika
salt and pepper
parsley (chopped)

Cut the meat into large cubes and toss in seasoned flour. Slice the onions, cube the potato, and cut the bacon up small. In a heavy saucepan melt the fat over a low heat. Fry the meat and onions until golden brown. Add the stock, bacon, seasonings and stir thoroughly. Cook slowly until the meat is tender. Remove the bouquet garni, stir well and check the seasoning. Add a little more stock if necessary and the potato. Boil gently until the potato is cooked. Take off the heat and add the red wine and lemon juice. Sprinkle with parsley and serve piping hot.

Serves 3–4

Baked Loin of Pork with Ginger Sauce

2 tablespoons ginger wine
3 pounds (boned weight) boneless pork loin
4 tablespoons salad oil
salt and pepper
¼ teaspoon thyme
¼ teaspoon rosemary
2 tablespoons lemon juice
8 ounces sliced onion
8 ounces sliced celery
1 teaspoon very finely minced fresh ginger
¼ pint single cream
2 tablespoons butter
2 tablespoons flour

Have the butcher tie the pork as for roasting. Place pork in a shallow pan or bowl. Pour oil over meat, sprinkle with salt and pepper. Rub the thyme and rosemary into the meat; add lemon juice, onion and celery. Toss ingredients. Cover bowl with clear plastic wrap and marinate overnight. Preheat oven at 375°F./

Gas 5. Place pork, with marinating vegetables, in a fireproof dish, discarding the liquid. Cover and bake for 2½–3 hours or until the pork is very tender. Pour off liquid from dish into container and skim fat from liquid. Keep pork warm. Pour liquid into saucepan, add minced ginger and cream. Bring to the boil. Mix butter and flour to a smooth paste, add to liquid and stir until sauce is thickened. Simmer for 5 minutes. Stir in ginger wine. Season with salt and pepper to taste. Serve sauce separately at table.

Serves 4–5

Calf's Sweetbreads with Madeira

3½ tablespoons Madeira
7 tablespoons dry white wine
3 calf's sweetbreads
2 carrots
7 ounces cooked ham
salt and pepper
butter

Plunge the sweetbreads into hot water and then remove the skin. Brown in a saucepan in butter, adding the diced carrots and the roughly cut ham. When they are all golden brown, pour in the Madeira and white wine. Season and stew for a good hour.

Serves 4–6

Gammon Rashers in Port

port
gamon rashers
orange juice
peppercorns

Place trimmed rashers in a casserole. Cover with port. Add 2 peppercorns for every ½ pound ham. Cover and cook in a slow oven till tender. Add the strained juice of half an orange for every tablespoon of wine left. Drain into a saucepan. Boil up and serve as gravy.

Serves 3–4

Ham in Cream Sauce

2 tablespoons port
6 slices of cooked ham
3 tomatoes
10 ounces mushrooms
7 ounces butter
1 pint double cream

In a frying pan heat the ham with part of the butter very quickly, but do not cook. Place the slices on a hot dish. Fry the halved tomatoes and separately sauté the mushrooms. Arrange the tomatoes and mushrooms alternately round the dish. Melt the rest of the butter in a saucepan. Add the fresh cream, salt and pepper, and cook without letting it come to the boil, stirring continuously with a wooden spoon. Add the port, and sprinkle the sauce over the ham just before serving.

Serves 6

Intoxicated Pork

chianti
loin of pork
salt and pepper
1–2 tablespoons oil
cloves of garlic
chopped parsley

Season the pork well with salt and pepper and brown it in the oil in a deep frying pan, with cloves of garlic to taste and chopped parsley. Add a generous supply of chianti and simmer the meat till the wine has reduced by half. To serve, put the meat on a hot dish and pour the sauce over.

Allow 1 chop per person

Kidneys with Stuffed Onions

1 tablespoon sherry
4 lamb's kidneys
6 large onions
¼ pound bacon
¼ pound mushrooms
¼ pint creamy milk
pepper and salt
¼ pound butter
1 pint beef stock
¼ pint tomato purée
2 pounds potatoes
½ tablespoon flour

Cook and cream the potatoes. Peel and rinse the onions and boil until soft. Strain and drain on a cloth. Remove the centre of the onions for use in the stuffing. Cut the kidneys into slices and braise them in a little butter, add the cleaned and sliced mushrooms and pepper and salt to taste. Stir over low heat, add the flour and mix well, pour in the stock and mix. Stir over the heat and bring to the boil, stirring all the time. When thickened, lower the heat and simmer for half an hour with the lid on, stirring once or twice. When cooked add the chopped up onion centres, the tomato purée and the sherry. Bring to the boil slowly for two minutes. Stuff the onions with this mixture and place them in a fireproof dish. Cut the bacon into strips and fry until crisp. Strain the bacon fat over the stuffed onions and keep the bacon strips hot. Place the onions in a medium hot oven (400°F./Gas 6) for 10–15 minutes. Spread the creamed potatoes on a serving dish and place the stuffed onions on top. Sprinkle the bacon strips around the dish.

Serves 4

Pork Chops Charcutière

½ cup dry white wine or dry vermouth
4 lean pork chops, 1 inch thick
salt and freshly ground black pepper
1 tablespoon vegetable oil
4 tablespoons shallots
1 tablespoon finely chopped onion
1 cup beef stock
1 tablespoon Dijon mustard
2 tablespoons butter
3 small gherkins (cut into strips)

Trim pork chops, leaving just a thin layer of fat. Sprinkle lightly with salt and pepper. Heat all in a large skillet and brown chops on both sides. Cook until done (about 30 minutes). Slit near bone to be sure chops are cooked. Transfer to warm dish and cover to keep warm. Add shallots and onion to skillet and cook, stirring, for 2 minutes. Slowly add wine and stir to dissolve brown particles in pan. Cook rapidly, stirring, until wine is reduced to ¼ cup. Reduce heat, slowly add hot bouillon. Cook, stirring, for 10 minutes. Mix mustard and butter together. Swirl into sauce. Add gherkins. Add chops and heat through. To serve, spoon some sauce over each chop and serve remaining sauce in a sauce-boat.

Serves 4

Pork Spareribs Hawaii

¼ pint dry or medium sherry
5 tablespoons red wine vinegar
3½ pounds pork spareribs cut into serving portions
salt and pepper
1 tablespoon cornflour
1 large tablespoon brown sugar
1 9-ounce can crushed pineapple (undrained)
2 tablespoons soya sauce
4–5 servings boiled sweet potatoes

Season the spareribs with salt and pepper. Arrange in a shallow baking pan meaty side up. Mix the cornflour and brown sugar in a saucepan. Stir in pineapple, vinegar, wine, and soya sauce; stir over medium heat until mixture boils and thickens. Pour sauce over the spareribs. Bake, uncovered, in a moderate oven (400°F./Gas 6) for 1–1¼ hours, basting occasionally. Arrange sweet potatoes around spareribs. Continue baking for about ½ hour, basting occasionally. Arrange on a heated dish and serve.

Serves 6

Noisettes of Lamb

1 glass Madeira
10 lamb noisettes
2 ounces butter
1½ pounds mushrooms
1 teaspoon meat extract
petits pois
1 tablespoon tomato purée
Worcestershire sauce
½ pint stock
salt and pepper

Have the butcher prepare the noisettes by cutting them from a loin of lamb, into 1½-inch slices. They should have a strip of fat fastened round them with a wooden toothpick.

Season the meat with salt and pepper and place in a pan. Put nuts of butter on them and grill for 5–6 minutes on each side, basting once or twice, until they are lightly browned. They should still be pink inside. Sprinkle a little Worcestershire sauce over the meat and put on a dish to keep hot. Pour the heated stock into the grilling pan and add the tomato purée, meat extract, Madeira and a nut of butter. Pour into another pan and boil until thick and slightly transparent. Strain the sauce over the lamb. While the meat is cooking, sauté the mushrooms in butter and cook the peas. Place the noisettes on a large serving dish and arrange the peas and mushrooms around them. Serve with redcurrant jelly.

Serves 4–5

Veal Kidneys with Mustard Sauce

¼ pint dry vermouth
4 veal kidneys (whole but with fat removed)
4 tablespoons butter
2 tablespoons minced shallots
1 tablespoon lemon juice
1½ tablespoons Dijon mustard
2 tablespoons soft butter
salt and pepper
3 tablespoons chopped parsley or *chives*

Heat butter in a shallow casserole or chafing dish. When foam subsides, roll kidneys in butter. Cook, uncovered, for about 10 minutes, over medium heat, turning every 2 minutes. When kidneys are light brown, firm, and slightly puffy, remove to a hot plate, cover, and keep warm. Add shallots to butter in casserole, and cook for 1–2 minutes. Add wine and lemon juice, and boil, stirring and scraping up browned particles, until wine is reduced by half. Mix mustard and 2 tablespoons of butter and swirl into wine. Add salt and pepper to taste. Cut kidneys crossways into ¼-inch slices. Sprinkle lightly with salt and pepper. Return kidneys to casserole. Stir over low heat only long enough to warm through. Do not allow sauce to boil. Sprinkle with chopped parsley or chives.

Serves 4

Escalope de Veau

1 gill white wine
6 veal cutlets (about 1 inch thick × 4 inches across)
½ pint chicken or veal stock
¼ pint cream
1 tablespoon nut oil
6 slices lemon
chopped capers
3½ ounces butter
8 anchovy fillets
flour
eggs for coating
fresh breadcrumbs
salt, pepper and sugar to taste

Flatten the cutlets and score lightly on both sides with a knife. Sprinkle with salt, dip in flour and coat with egg and breadcrumbs. Fry in oil and 3 ounces butter over gentle heat until light brown on each side. Add the heated stock with half the wine and place in a medium hot oven (350°F./Gas 4) to cook for 15–20 minutes. Place on a dish and then add the rest of the wine, the cream, sugar and two anchovy fillets to the sauce. Stir over a low heat and mix well, adding a little more stock if necessary. Strain the sauce, which should be fairly thick, into a pan and add the rest of the butter. Bring to the boil and pour over the veal. Arrange the anchovy fillets in a ring in the centre of the lemon slices and fill with chopped capers, and place a slice on each escalope.

Serves 6

Lamb Kidneys Sautéed with White Wine

3½ tablespoons white wine
2 kidneys per person
6 small mushrooms
lemon juice
1 level tablespoon flour
butter
bay leaf
salt and pepper

Remove the fat and skin from the kidneys and slice thinly. Melt the butter in a frying pan and, when very hot, put in the sliced kidneys and bay leaf, and season with salt and pepper. Cook for a few minutes on brisk heat, shaking the pan, and turning the kidneys with a spoon. When nearly done (about 8–10 minutes), sprinkle with a little flour, stir it in well, then remove the pan from the heat, and add the white wine. Replace the pan on the heat, stir for 2–3 minutes and add the mushrooms, by bringing a little salted water, the juice of half a lemon and 1 ounce butter to the boil, adding the mushrooms, then boiling rapidly for 4–5 minutes. Add to the kidney mixture, stir, and serve very hot.

Allow 2 kidneys per person

Sauté of Liver

1 tablespoon Madeira
6–8 ounces calf or *lamb's liver*
1 large onion
1 pound mushrooms (sliced)
2 ounces butter
¼ pint stock or *water*
1 ounce flour
¼ pint cream
pepper and salt

Cut the liver into strips and chop the onion finely. Put the butter in a saucepan on moderate heat and brown the liver. Add the onions and lower the heat. Add the sliced mushrooms and stir. Sprinkle the flour over the mixture and stir the ingredients together. Add the heated stock or water a little at a time and season. Add the wine, stir well and bring to the boil. Lower the heat and simmer for 15 minutes. Add the cream, stir, and simmer for a further 10 minutes. (A border of boiled rice goes well with this dish.)

Serves 2–3

Rump Steak en Casserole

1 gill claret
2 pounds rump steak
seasoned flour
¾ pint stock
butter
2 large onions
salt
2 pounds potatoes
½ pound mushrooms (peeled and sliced)
¼ teaspoon white pepper
½ teaspoon browning

Have the steak cut into individual portions and pound well. Turn the steaks in seasoned flour. Peel and cut the potatoes and onions in thick slices. Peel and slice the mushrooms and fry in butter. Mix the stock with the wine and browning. Grease a casserole with 1 ounce butter. Place the potatoes on the bottom of the dish, cover with a layer of onions, then place the steaks and mushrooms on top. Finish with another layer of potatoes and sprinkle with salt. Dot with pieces of butter and pour over the wine and stock. Cover with a lid and braise on top of the cooker or in a low oven (400°F./Gas 6) for 2½ hours.

Serves 4–5

Stewed Mutton

1 tablespoon sherry
2 pounds leg of mutton with skin
1 dessertspoon soy sauce
1 ounce dried orange peel
1 piece ginger or *1 clove garlic*
1 teaspoon salt

Cut meat into neat shapes and simmer in 2 pints water on a very low heat with the lid on the pan. Add the sherry, ginger or garlic and orange peel when it has been brought to the boil. Stir a few times during the process of cooking (about 50 minutes). Season with soy sauce before serving.

Serves 4

Veal Sauté

6 tablespoons white wine
2 pounds lean veal
1 pint of stock
1 large onion
1 clove garlic
1 pound chopped tomatoes
3 tablespoons oil
½ ounce flour
12 pickling onions
¾ pound small mushrooms (chopped)
salt and pepper

Put the oil in a saucepan and, when very hot, add the sliced onion and veal, cut into 2-inch lengths, after removing all fat and gristle. Allow both the onion and the veal to become brown. Then pour out the oil, add the white wine and let this reduce almost completely. Cover with the hot stock and add the chopped tomatoes, the garlic and mixed herbs. Bring to the boil and simmer very gently for 1½ hours. Now put the pieces of veal in another saucepan, reduce the sauce by about ⅓ and strain it over the veal. Add the pickling onions, lightly browned in butter, and the mushrooms, already chopped and cooked in a little butter, and simmer all together for another 15 minutes.

Serves 6

Lemon Veal with Olives

5 or *6 tablespoons dry Marsala*
3 pounds boneless veal (rolled and tied)
2 tablespoons grated lemon rind (use fresh lemons)
1 clove garlic (finely minced)
¾ teaspoon salt
¼ teaspoon pepper
½ teaspoon dried rosemary (crushed)
¼ teaspoon dried sweet basil
3 tablespoons olive oil
½ cup stoned ripe olives (sliced)

Mix lemon rind, garlic, salt, pepper, rosemary and basil. Divide this mixture in half. Untie and unroll the veal and rub the inner surface with one half of the flavouring mixture. Re-roll and re-tie. Rub the remaining mixture all over the outside of the veal.

Heat the olive oil over medium high heat in a heavy casserole large enough to hold the veal. Brown the veal slightly. Pour the wine over the veal, reduce the heat to low, cover tightly and simmer for about 1½ hours, or until it is fork tender, but not too soft. Turn the veal occasionally and be careful not to overcook. When done, remove the veal to a hot platter and keep warm. There should be quite a lot of liquid in the casserole. Increase the heat and boil until liquid is reduced to about half. Add the sliced olives and heat through. The sauce should thicken somewhat on being reduced. Slice the veal and spoon the sauce over it.

Serves 6

Beef Hotpot

1 glass dry red wine
1 pound fat soup beef
¾ pound lean soup beef
1½ pints water
3 pounds old carrots
3 pounds potatoes
10 ounces onions
salt

Wash the meat and place in a pan of warm salted water. Bring to the boil and simmer for 2 hours. Add the finely chopped, peeled carrots to the stock after the 2 hours. Add the peeled potatoes and the chopped onions after another ½ hour and simmer until the vegetables are very tender. If necessary, add more water during the process of cooking, adding the wine when the meat is half cooked. When the dish is ready, all liquid should have evaporated. Remove the meat from the saucepan to a hot dish. Mash all the vegetables with a wooden spoon and put on the dish with the meat.

Serves 6

Pork Schnitzel

1 pound loin of pork fillet
(½ inch thick)
egg and breadcrumbs
stock
salt and cayenne pepper
flour
pork fat

Tomato sauce:
1 large onion
1 knob butter
½ pound tomatoes
1 teaspoon mustard
1 glass sherry
seasoning

Pepper and salt the pork. Dip in flour, egg and breadcrumbs and fry slowly in pork fat until golden brown (allow about ½ hour). Remove and place in the centre of a serving dish and keep hot. Strain the liquor after having whisked out the pan with a little stock, and pour over the pork.

Tomato sauce: brown the chopped onion in butter, add tomatoes, allow to simmer for 10 minutes and sieve. Dissolve the mustard in the sherry, add to the mixture and season. Serve in a sauce-boat.

Serves 3

Poultry and Game

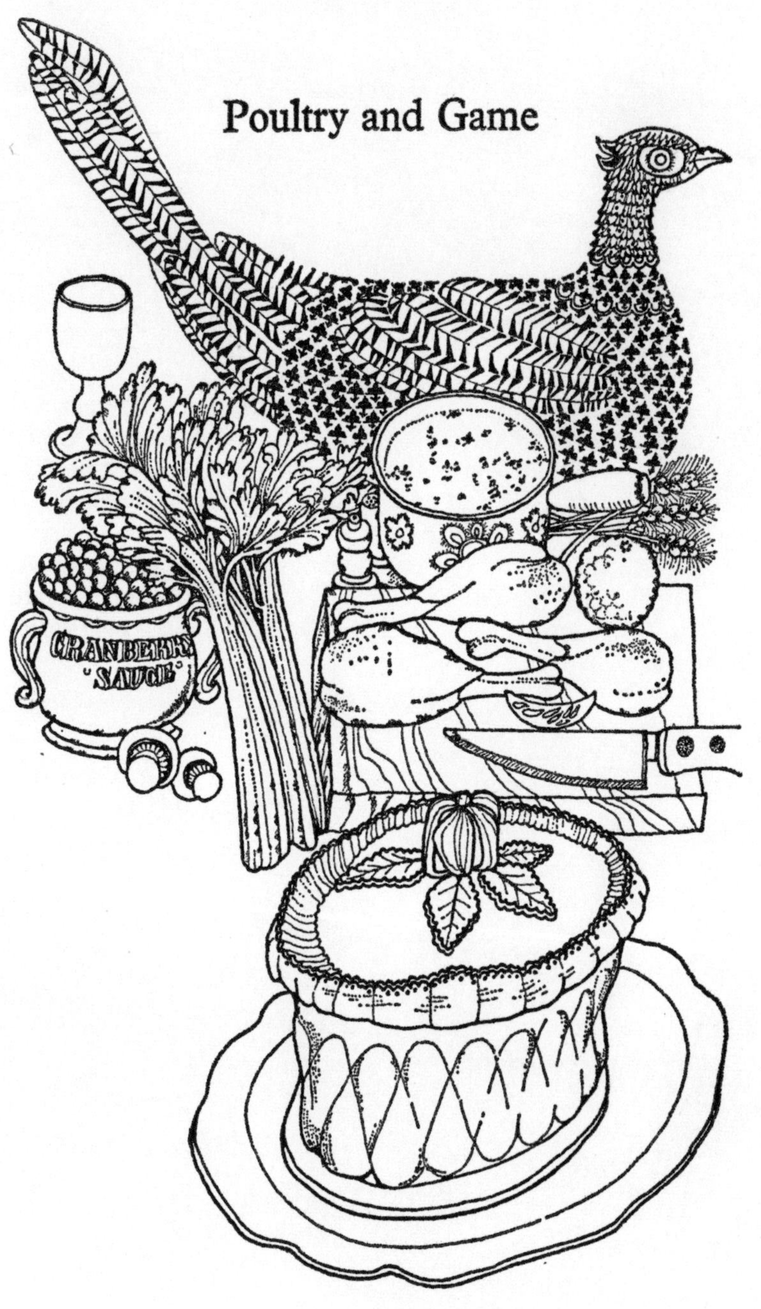

Wine Pointers for Poultry and Game

1. Flavour gravy to accompany any roast game with sherry, Madeira or port, to taste.
2. Game essence, obtained after draining fat from baking tin in which game has been roasted, can be turned into delicious gravy: stir in enough sour cream to give you a slightly thick sauce, then stir in a little wine to taste. Strain into a hot sauce-boat.
3. Stuff young grouse with brown breadcrumbs soaked in port. Roast birds upside down.
4. Flavour bread sauce intended to accompany game with Madeira or sherry to taste.

Chicken in Wine and Cream

4 tablespoons dry white wine
2 tablespoons dry sherry
1 meaty chicken
2 tablespoons butter
juice of half a lemon
bouquet garni
1 small onion
mushrooms
1 cup double cream

Cut the chicken into serving pieces and cook them in a large shallow saucepan with two generous tablespoons butter, the chopped onion and salt and pepper. Turn the chicken several times and then cover and place over a low heat so that the meat will steam and cook slowly for about 20 minutes. Moisten the chicken with the wine and sherry. Add the bouquet garni and cook for another 15 minutes very gently, or until the chicken is tender. In the meantime, place the cream over brisk heat to reduce, and stir occasionally. Add the juice of half a lemon, and salt and pepper. Place the chicken in a serving dish with the mushrooms cooked in a little white wine and water. Add the cream to the juices in the pan and stir in a few drops of sherry. Strain the sauce over the chicken through a fine sieve, and serve very hot.

Serves 5–6

Pheasant Italienne

1 gill Marsala
2 young pheasants
5 tablespoons olive oil
1 clove garlic
seasoned flour
salt and pepper
4 small onions
1 green pepper
1 gill consommé
1 pound sliced mushrooms
1 10½-ounce can tomatoes
marjoram

Have the pheasants cut into portions and dip into seasoned flour. Pour the olive oil into a deep heavy frying pan and, when it is hot, put in the pheasant and brown on all sides. Slice the seeded green pepper lengthways and mix with the onions and garlic, peeled and chopped, the tomatoes, a good pinch of marjoram and add this mixture to the pheasant. Now add the consommé and the Marsala. Cover and simmer for about 1 hour. Add the sliced mushrooms and simmer for approximately ½ an hour.

Serves 6

Chicken Caesar

1¾ pints good red wine
1 3-pound chicken
4 ounces diced lean bacon
10 small onions, whole
½ pound butter
½ pound mushrooms (quartered or button)
bouquet garni
1 tablespoon flour
salt and pepper
croûtons

Prepare and cut the chicken into pieces. Put some butter, diced bacon and onions in a deep skillet and brown for 5 minutes. Add the mushrooms and sauté for 5 minutes. Then remove all the ingredients from the skillet. Fry the chicken lightly in butter until golden brown (about 10 minutes). Season with salt and pepper and a bouquet garni. Add the bacon, mushrooms and onions, and sauté for 5 minutes. Sprinkle with flour and mix well. Pour the red wine over the chicken and simmer for about 35 minutes. Serve very hot with croûtons fried in butter.

Serves 6

Chicken in Red Wine

1¾ pints red wine
1 plump chicken (3½ pounds)
3½ tablespoons butter
10 very small whole onions
4 ounces diced fat bacon
salt and pepper
1 clove garlic (crushed)
bouquet garni
sprig of savory
½ large teaspoon flour
5½ tablespoons beef or chicken stock
croûtons

Cut the chicken into small pieces and fry lightly for 10 minutes in the butter with the onions, bacon, garlic, bouquet garni and savory. Sprinkle with the flour and simmer for 5 minutes. Add the red wine and the stock and cook very slowly until done. The cooking time will depend on the age of the chicken. When done, put the chicken pieces into a casserole. Keep hot. Dilute the sauce with a little red wine. Beat well, season to taste, strain carefully through a sieve over the pieces of chicken and add a good pinch of pepper. Cover and simmer for 5 minutes. If desired, serve with croûtons fried in butter.

Serves 4–5

Chicken à la King

¾ gill Madeira
¾ pound chopped cooked chicken
1½ pints single cream
½ pint chicken broth
2 egg yolks
salt and pepper
4 tablespoons flour
4 ounces butter
½ pound sliced mushrooms
1 green pepper
2 tablespoons chopped tinned pimento
Melba toast

Make a white sauce as follows: Melt 2 ounces butter in a saucepan and stir in four tablespoons flour. Add the chicken broth and cream and, stirring constantly, cook until the mixture is thick. Now add salt and white pepper to taste, and the chopped cooked chicken. In another saucepan melt 2 ounces butter and put into it the thinly sliced fresh mushrooms. In about 10 minutes when these are tender, add them to the chicken and cream sauce. Stirring constantly, simmer for about 10 minutes; then add the two lightly beaten egg yolks. Reduce the heat and for about 1 minute stir constantly. Remove from the stove and stir in 2 tablespoons of canned chopped pimento and the Madeira. Stir and serve on Melba toast.

Serves 4–5

Rabbit with Paprika

¼ pint dry sherry
1 young rabbit
seasoned flour
4 tablespoons butter
salt and pepper
2 tomatoes
3 medium onions
1 clove garlic
½ pint sour cream
1½ tablespoons paprika

Have the rabbit cut into portions and toss them in seasoned flour. Melt the butter in heavy frying pan and put in the peeled and chopped onions. Cook slowly for about ½ an hour, taking care that they do not burn. Add the paprika and, stirring constantly, cook for another 15 minutes. Add the pieces of rabbit, the garlic, the cut up tomatoes and the dry sherry. Cover, and let all simmer for about an hour, or until the rabbit is tender. A few minutes before serving add the sour cream. Mix well, test for seasoning, and allow to simmer long enough to heat the sour cream. Serve very hot.

Serves 4–5

Pigeons in Dry Vermouth

½ pint dry French vermouth or *similar Italian dry vermouth*
4 young pigeons
¾ medium cup breadcrumbs
¼ medium cup cashew nuts
4 slices bacon
1 slice onion
½ medium cup chopped mushrooms
¼ medium cup chopped apple
salt and pepper
buttered toast
3 tablespoons butter

Melt the butter in a saucepan and, when hot, add the finely chopped onion and the chopped mushrooms. Sauté until tender, and then add the finely chopped cashew nuts, the chopped apple and the breadcrumbs. Add salt and pepper to taste and enough of the dry vermouth to bind all together, after mixing well. Stuff the pigeons with this mixture and place them in a roasting pan with 2 half slices of bacon on each breast. Pour the vermouth into the pan and roast in a very hot oven, basting frequently, for about 20 minutes, or until the birds are tender. Place each pigeon on a slice of hot buttered toast and pour the liquor in the pan over them.

Serves 4

Chicken with Rosemary

1 gill Marsala
4–5 chicken portions
salt and pepper (freshly ground)
about 4 tablespoons olive oil
rosemary
2 cloves garlic
oregano

Put the olive oil into a heavy frying pan and add the crushed cloves of garlic. When hot, place the portions of chicken, rubbed with salt and freshly ground pepper, in the pan and brown on both sides. Sprinkle the chicken with the rosemary and oregano and slowly add the Marsala. Cover and simmer for about 30–35 minutes, when the chicken should be tender. If necessary, add more Marsala to prevent the contents of the pan from becoming dry. Serve very hot.

Serves 4

Savoury Chicken

¼ pint white wine
4 chicken joints
1½ ounces butter
salt and pepper
1 tablespoon oil
4 ripe tomatoes
1 green pepper
2 ounces bacon
4 ounces mushrooms
parsley

Sprinkle the chicken with salt. Fry the joints in the butter and oil, already heated in a heavy pan, till golden brown on both sides. Meanwhile discard the seeds from the green pepper and cut into thin strips, and skin and slice the tomatoes. Dice the bacon and chop the mushrooms. Add the mushrooms, bacon, tomatoes, pepper and wine to the chicken in the pan. Replace lid and simmer for 25 minutes. Remove the chicken and place on a serving dish and keep hot. Now reduce the sauce to coating thickness by boiling fast, without the lid, for a few minutes. Season the sauce to taste and pour over the chicken. Sprinkle with chopped parsley.

Serves 4

Creamed Turkey

3 tablespoons Madeira or *sherry*
½ pint milk
2 tablespoons flour
salt and pepper
celery salt
1–1¼ pounds diced cooked turkey
3 tablespoons butter
2 hard-boiled eggs
cream
cayenne

Melt butter in the top of a double boiler. Stir in the flour and when frothy draw the pan to the side and stir in the milk. Return to the heat and stir till boiling and well blended. Season to taste with salt, pepper, celery salt and cayenne. Add turkey, minced egg yolk and chopped egg white and stir till piping hot; add the Madeira or sherry and a little cream. Serve either on hot buttered toast or fried bread.

Serves 4

Chicken with Almonds

- *½ teacup dry white wine*
- *¼ teacup sherry*
- *3 teacups sliced cooked chicken*
- *1 teacup chicken stock*
- *1 tablespoon minced onion*
- *¼ teacup raisins*
- *3 egg yolks*
- *3 tablespoons butter*
- *1 teacup medium white sauce (see below)*
- *1 clove*
- *½ teacup thick cream* or *evaporated milk*
- *¼ bay leaf*
- *½ teacup minced blanched almonds*
- *salt and pepper*

For medium white sauce:

- *2 tablespoons butter*
- *2 tablespoons flour*
- *1 cupful rich milk*
- *½ teaspoon salt*
- *⅛ teaspoon pepper*

Sauté the onion in the butter until slightly brown. Add the wine, chicken stock, seasoning, clove, bay leaf and white sauce. Cook for 5 minutes stirring until smooth. Add chicken, raisins and almonds and heat thoroughly; add sherry and egg yolks (previously beaten) with cream or evaporated milk, cook 1 minute, stirring constantly. Serve at once.

For the sauce: melt the butter and add the flour, stir till smooth and add the milk and seasonings. Cook for 5 minutes or so until thickened.

Rice goes well with this dish.

Serves 4

Pheasant as in Normandy

1 gill dry French vermouth or *similar Italian dry vermouth*
1 pheasant
6 cooking apples
butter
3 tablespoons single cream
salt and pepper

Fry the pheasant all over in butter. Toss in another pan, also in butter, the peeled and cored apples cut in slices. Put a layer of the apples into a buttered casserole, place the bird on top and put the rest of the apple round it. Sprinkle over this the dry vermouth and the cream and cook, covered, in a moderate oven until tender.

Serves 4

Salmi of Duck

1 bottle red wine
1 duck
3 onions
2½ ounces smoked bacon
3½ ounces butter
salt and pepper
bouquet garni
6 fried croûtons

Cut the duck into joints and fry until golden brown in a saucepan with the blanched bacon, cut into small pieces. Add the thickly sliced onions. Take the duck joints out of the saucepan. Blend a little butter and flour and cook for a few minutes until brown. Wet with the wine, season with salt and pepper, add a bouquet garni and the duck joints and cook for at least ¾ hour (cooking depends on the size of the duck, and also, more especially, on its age). Place the joints on a hot dish. Strain the sauce adding the crushed raw liver and the rest of the butter to thicken. Pour over the duck and garnish with the fried croûtons.

Serves 4

Chicken with White Sauce

1 glass white wine
1 chicken (3–4 pounds)
5 ounces butter
1 tablespoon flour
1 glass water
½ pint cream
bouquet garni
1 clove garlic
6 little onions
2 egg yolks
salt and pepper

Cut the chicken into joints and fry in melted butter in the saucepan without letting it brown. Remove from the pan. Put fresh butter in the pan with the flour and make a white roux. Add the bouquet garni, water and white wine, onions and the crushed clove of garlic. Season with salt and pepper and add the chicken. Cover and cook for about half an hour. Remove the chicken and keep warm. Remove the bouquet garni. Beat the two egg yolks in the cup of cream and add to the sauce, taking care not to bring to the boil. Add a few drops of lemon juice. Put the chicken back in the sauce and serve very hot. This dish can be served with mushrooms browned in butter with parsley, shallots and white wine and then cooked for ½ hour in peppered cream.

Serves 6

Duckling en Casserole

1 gill Chablis or Graves
1 duckling
2 ounces fat bacon
1 gill white stock
1 small carrot (sliced)
1 stalk celery (chopped)
1 teaspoon lemon juice
1 orange
½ teaspoon shredded lemon rind
½ teaspoon shredded orange rind
1 small onion
2 ounces butter

Cut the bacon into small squares and lay in the casserole. Chop and add the onion, the chopped celery and the sliced carrot. Lay the duckling on top, having spread with the butter. Cover. Cook for about 20 minutes. Uncover and brown in a moderate oven. Remove the duckling to a hot dish. Strain off the fat. Add the stock and wine and cook quickly for 10 minutes to reduce the sauce. Add the lemon juice and strained orange juice. Cook the shredded lemon and orange rind for 6 minutes in boiling water. Strain and add the rind to the sauce. Pour over the duckling.

Serves 4–5

Chicken Alsace

1 pint dry white wine
1 4-pound chicken
3 egg yolks
½ pint double cream
1 tablespoon flour
1 onion (chopped)
½ pint water
1 bay leaf
2 cloves garlic (chopped)
3–4 tablespoons butter
salt and pepper
pinch nutmeg
2 cloves
mushrooms

Cut the chicken into portions. Salt and pepper them, then sauté in 2–3 tablespoons butter in a wide saucepan over a medium heat until golden brown. Add the chopped onion and garlic, bay leaf and cloves. Put in the wine and the water. Simmer until the drumsticks are tender. Remove on to a dish and keep hot. Simmer the liquor for 5–6 minutes to reduce, and strain. In a second saucepan melt a generous tablespoon of butter, blend in the flour and gradually stir in the chicken bouillon. Add the cream and the nutmeg and thicken by pouring into the beaten egg yolks and gradually reheating, stirring all the time with a whisk (do not allow to boil). Pour the sauce over the chicken and garnish with sautéed mushroom caps.

Noodles or rice are good accompaniments for this dish.

Serves 4–5

Roast Duck in Claret Sauce (*page* 90)

Tomato Salad (*page* 101) and Lombardy Eggs (*page* 26)

Chicken Algarve

1 gill white wine
1 chicken (2½–3 pounds)
2½ ounces butter
1 tablespoon nut oil
1 tablespoon tomato purée
salt, pepper and sugar to taste
flour
¼ pint cream
½ pint chicken stock
8 stuffed olives

Cut the legs from the chicken, remove the breast and remove the skin. Cut the legs in two at the joint and cut each breast in two slantwise. In a saucepan melt 2 ounces butter and the oil, dip the chicken pieces in flour and fry over a gentle heat. Add salt and pepper. Allow the legs to cook for a little longer. When cooked, place the chicken on a serving dish. Add stock to the pan, then the wine, tomato purée and a pinch of sugar. Boil to reduce to half the quantity. Lower the heat and add the cream and the remainder of the butter. Strain the sauce over the chicken and garnish with the olives.

Serves 4

Roast Duckling with Giblet Sauce

2 tablespoons port or *Burgundy*
2 small ducklings (about 4 pounds each)
salt and pepper
thyme
4 small onions (2 sliced, 2 coarsely chopped)
3 small carrots
herb bouquet (2 parsley sprigs, small bay leaf, ¼ teaspoon sage)
1½ cups beef bouillon
duck gizzard, heart and neck (cut into 1-inch pieces, reserving liver for later cooking)
2 tablespoons oil

Preheat oven to 425°F./Gas 7. Season duck cavities with salt, pepper, and a pinch of thyme. Stuff each with a small sliced onion. Tie legs, wings, and neck skin tightly to body and place breast-up in a shallow roasting pan. Slice two of the carrots and one onion and sprinkle around the birds. Cook until lightly browned, about 15 minutes. Reduce oven to 350°F./Gas 4, turn the ducks breast-down and roast for 30 minutes. Take care that fat does not brown. Turn ducks breast-up and cook until done (about 30 minutes). (*Note:* duck is medium rare if juices from thigh run pale rosy when meat is pricked, and well done when juices run pale yellow.) While duck is roasting, prepare stock for sauce. Cut up and brown the giblets, 1 carrot and 1 onion in hot oil. Add the bouillon and herb bouquet. Simmer until giblets are very tender, for about 1 hour, adding water if necessary.

When duck is done, drain cavity juices into stock, and place duck on a warm platter. Place in the oven, turned off and with door left ajar, while preparing sauce. Pour juices remaining in roasting pan into a bowl, and remove as much fat as possible. Add these juices to stock. Remove herb bouquet from stock, then pour stock back into roasting pan, place over high heat and cook, stirring and scraping browned particles from bottom of pan. Crush the vegetables. Add wine and chopped liver, and cook until liver is just done. Correct seasonings and serve poured over duck.

Serves 6

Stewed Duck in Claret

1 pint claret
1 duck
2 large onions
3½ ounces fat pork
1 large tablespoon olive oil
1 sprig parsley
thyme
a small piece bay leaf
clove of garlic
7 ounces mushrooms
salt and pepper

Put the jointed duck in an earthenware casserole and season with salt, pepper and the spices. Add the onions and the claret. Allow to stand for a few hours. Put the oil and pork fat in another casserole and, when hot, put in the pieces of duck and brown them for about 15–20 minutes. Add the wine, etc. in which they have marinated, the garlic and the mushrooms. Simmer on gentle heat for 1–1½ hours. Serve in the casserole in which they were cooked.

Serves 4–5

Rabbit in White Wine

¾ pint white wine
1 young rabbit (5–6 pounds)
½ pound lean gammon
18 pickling onions
1 pound mushrooms
1 tablespoon flour
½ pint stock
lard, butter or *oil*
1 clove garlic
salt and pepper

Carve the rabbit into neat joints. Melt a few tablespoons of lard, butter or oil in a saucepan and, when hot, add the pieces of rabbit and season with salt and pepper. Cook till browned evenly on all sides. Sprinkle with the flour and let this brown also. Now add the wine and stock, bring to the boil, cover and simmer for ½ hour. Add the bacon, diced, the onions, both having been lightly browned in butter, and the mushrooms and garlic. Cover and simmer for another ½ hour. Serve in a fairly deep dish, with the garnish and, if desired, a few croûtons of fried bread.

Serves 6–8

Duck with Macaroni

1 gill red wine
1 young duck
1 pound tomatoes
butter or *oil*
salt and pepper
mixed herbs
salt and pepper
macaroni (from a packet, or made as below)

Chop the tomatoes and place them in a pan with a little butter or oil. Cook till soft then add the duck, the wine and herbs, and season with salt and pepper. Chop the duck liver very finely and add it to the sauce. Simmer for 1½ hours, and before serving mix in the macaroni.

To make your own macaroni, you require:

4 whole eggs and the yolks of 1 or 2
1 pound flour
pinch of salt

Mix the eggs and the flour and work into a firm dough. Roll out very thinly and allow to stand for about 1 hour to dry thoroughly. Cut into strips just under ½-inch wide and cook in a large saucepan of boiling water, with salt added, for a few minutes. Drain thoroughly.

Serves 4–5

Hare in Red Wine

1½ pints red wine
1 hare
butter
1 pound small mushrooms
6–8 small sausages
salt and pepper

Joint the hare and brown the pieces in butter in an earthenware casserole. Season with salt and pepper, cover with the red wine. Cover and simmer very gently in the oven for 1½–2 hours. Thirty minutes before serving, add 6–8 small sausages, lightly browned in butter, and 1 pound small mushrooms. Finish cooking and serve in the casserole.

Serves 5–6

Roast Duck with Claret Sauce

2 dessert apples
2 cloves
1 pound prunes
1 duck
seasoning

For the sauce:

1 glass claret
½ pint stock
½ cup prune juice
1 tablespoon flour
1 dessertspoon orange marmalade

Core and quarter the apples and insert the cloves. Soak the prunes overnight in cold water and remove the stones. Season the duck generously with salt and pepper, inside and out. Rub the liver from the bird all over the breast. Stuff the duck with the apples and half of the prunes. Cover the breast with foil and roast in a hot oven for 1 hour 20 minutes. After ½ hour lower the heat and baste occasionally. Before 15 minutes of the cooking time remove the foil and let the duck brown without basting. While the duck is cooking, simmer the remaining ½ pound prunes in water until soft. Then add a pinch of salt and keep simmering on a low heat. When the duck is cooked remove from the oven, place on a hot dish to keep warm and skim the fat from the gravy in the pan.

For the sauce, stir the flour in the skimmed gravy until smooth, add the stock and simmer for 10 minutes. Add the prune juice, half the glass of claret and the marmalade. Season to taste, strain and keep hot. To garnish, pour a tablespoon of the fat from the duck on to the strained prunes, add the rest of the claret and simmer for a few minutes so that the prunes become glazed. Arrange them round the duck.

Serves 3

Duck in Claret

1 pint claret
1 large duckling
3½ ounces pork fat
1 large tablespoon olive oil
¾ pound small mushrooms
2 large onions
a few sprigs of parsley
a few sprigs of thyme
a small bay leaf
1 clove garlic
salt and pepper
ribbon macaroni (if desired)

Joint the duck, place in an earthenware casserole and season with the salt, pepper and mixed spices. Add the sliced onions, the herbs, and red wine. Leave to stand for a few hours. Now put the oil and pork fat in another casserole and, when hot, add the pieces of duck, which should have been carefully dried in a cloth. Cook for about 15–20 minutes, till evenly browned on all sides. Add the wine, etc., in which the duck has marinated, and the garlic. Simmer on very gentle heat or in the oven (at 375°F./Gas 5) with the lid on the casserole, for 1–1½ hours. Thirty minutes before serving, put the peeled mushrooms in the casserole. This dish should be highly seasoned with salt and pepper. Serve in the casserole with, if desired, the plain ribbon macaroni (boiled, drained, tossed in a little butter and seasoned with salt and pepper).

Serves 4–5

Burgundy Baked Chicken

½ pint Burgundy or *other dry red wine*
1 chicken (cut into 8 pieces)
¼ pint nut oil (not olive oil)
1 medium onion (coarsely chopped)
2 cloves garlic (minced)
¼ teaspoon oregano
½ teaspoon salt
2 tablespoons lemon juice

Preheat oven to 350°F./Gas 4. Pour oil into a large skillet and heat over high heat until very hot, almost smoking. Add chicken pieces and sauté until a rich golden brown. Remove chicken pieces, drain on paper towels and place in a small, covered roasting pan. Remove all except 2 tablespoons of oil from the frying pan. Lower heat, add onion, garlic, oregano, salt, and lemon juice. Simmer over low heat until onion is soft and yellow, about 5 minutes. Sprinkle onion over chicken. Cover and bake for ½ hour (at 350°F./Gas 4). Correct seasoning. Bring wine to the boil and pour over chicken. Cook, uncovered, for 10 minutes longer on the top of the cooker.

Serves 6–8

Vegetables and Salads

THE ACCOMPANYING dishes of a meal can often make the difference between the mediocre and the superlative. In this section, there are some unusual mushroom recipes and a piquant Pickled Peaches recipe, all brought to life with the addition of wine.

Madeira Spinach

1 gill Madeira
2 pounds fresh spinach
1 gill sour cream
1 teaspoon lime juice
4 tablespoons butter
1 teaspoon Worcestershire sauce
¼ pound fresh mushrooms
salt
pepper (freshly ground)

Wash the spinach quickly in warm water and then several times in cold water. Put the spinach in 1 gill of salted water, cover, and cook for about 10 minutes over a low heat, or until tender. Remove and drain, then put it through a mincer, using the finest blade. Now put the spinach in a saucepan with 2 tablespoons butter, the Worcestershire sauce, sour cream, lime juice, salt and freshly ground pepper. Beat this well and keep warm. In a separate saucepan melt 2 tablespoons butter and sauté the sliced mushrooms for about 8 minutes. Add the mushrooms to the spinach and sour cream, and then add the Madeira. Mix all together and simmer for 2–3 minutes over medium heat.

Artichokes in White Wine

½ pint dry white wine
6 small globe artichokes
a small onion (chopped)
pinch of tarragon
1 tablespoon olive oil
1 clove garlic (chopped)
2 teaspoons salt

Trim the tops of the artichokes and the stems, and take off a few of the outer leaves. In a deep casserole put 1 tablespoon olive oil, the onion, the garlic, a pinch of tarragon and the salt. Put the artichokes upright in the casserole and pour the dry white wine over them. Cover tightly and simmer slowly for 45 minutes. Add a little more wine and olive oil if necessary. Remove when the hearts are tender, pour over the sauce, and serve.

Stewed Red Cabbage

1 glass port
4 cooking apples
4 ounces castor sugar
1 tablespoon caraway seeds (optional)
2 whole cloves
1 medium onion
1 medium red cabbage
½ pint vinegar
2 heaped tablespoons butter
1 tablespoon redcurrant jelly
salt and cayenne

Trim, wash and shred the cabbage. Soak in salted water for 1 hour. Drain well. Place in a saucepan. Add the butter, and enough water to cover. Stir in the peeled, sliced apples, cloves, caraway seeds, sugar, sliced and peeled onion, redcurrant jelly, salt and cayenne (to taste). Cover and simmer for 2 hours, then add vinegar and cover and simmer for another hour. Stir in the port. Serve with roast duck, goose or pork.

Jerusalem Artichokes

white wine
2 pounds Jerusalem artichokes
1 large onion
garlic (if desired)
bouquet garni
a pinch of mixed spices
stock
salt and pepper
butter or lard

Cook the sliced onion in hot butter or lard until it browns. Then add the peeled artichokes, cut in quarters, the herbs, garlic, spices, salt and pepper. Cover with equal parts of stock and white wine and simmer until the artichokes are tender.

Pickled Peaches

(Pickled peaches can hardly be termed a vegetable, but they make an excellent accompaniment to hot or cold ham.)

½ pint white wine
3 pounds peaches
1½ pounds sugar
½ ounce cinnamon
½ ounce allspice
½ ounce cloves
½ ounce mace
½ nutmeg

The peaches should be peeled and put in a pan with alternate layers of sugar, spices and wine. Bring to the boil and simmer for 5 minutes. Remove the fruit from the pan, pack into jars, simmer the syrup till it begins to thicken and pour it over the fruit. Cover with airtight lids.

Sauerkraut in White Wine

½ pint dry white wine
1 quart sauerkraut (drained)
2 tablespoons butter
1 small onion (minced)
1 cooking apple (chopped)
1 teaspoon caraway seeds
1 cup chicken stock

Sauté the onion in butter until light brown. Add to sauerkraut with apple and caraway seed, and turn into a greased casserole. Add stock and white wine. Bake, covered, in a medium oven for 45 minutes–1½ hours (for a shorter time if the sauerkraut is canned, a longer time if bulk).

Note: If the sauerkraut seems excessively salty before cooking, rinse with cold water. This method of preparing sauerkraut makes it particularly suitable for serving with pork, roast duck or goose, or grilled pork chops.

Sweet Potatoes

1 tablespoon dry French vermouth
2 pounds sweet potatoes
1 tablespoon butter
1 tablespoon cream
pinch of cayenne pepper

Boil in the same way as ordinary potatoes, add the butter, dry French vermouth, cream and pepper and beat very thoroughly.

Mushrooms in Madeira

1 gill Madeira
1 pound medium-sized mushrooms
1 ounce flour
2 ounces butter
salt and pepper
½ pint stock
1–2 sprigs parsley
1–2 sprigs thyme
1 small bay leaf
croûtons

Melt the butter in a saucepan and add the flour, working to a smooth paste and letting it brown slightly. Then add gradually ½ pint boiling stock, stirring well, the parsley, thyme and bay leaf. Season with a little salt and pepper. Remove the stalks and peel from the mushrooms and put them into the sauce and simmer for 30–35 minutes, depending on the size of the mushrooms. A few minutes before serving, add 1 gill Madeira. Put on a hot dish and garnish with croûtons of fried bread.

Devilled Mushrooms

3 tablespoons dry white wine
shallot or onion
½ pound or more of peeled mushrooms
6 tablespoons tarragon vinegar
½ pint good stock
½ ounce flour
½ ounce butter
1 teaspoon made mustard
salt
dash of cayenne

Into a small saucepan put 1 teaspoon finely chopped shallot or onion with 6 tablespoons tarragon vinegar, 3 tablespoons of dry white wine and on high heat reduce by half. Add ½ pint of stock, ½ ounce butter worked into ½ ounce flour, and stir well. Season with 1 teaspoon made mustard, a dash of cayenne pepper and salt. Simmer for 10 minutes. Then put the sauce into a larger saucepan and add ½ pound or more of peeled mushrooms, which have already been lightly cooked in butter. Stir well and simmer for a few minutes without boiling.

Mushrooms Espagnole

½ tumbler white wine
1 pound peeled mushrooms
4 tablespoons olive oil
salt and pepper
1–2 cloves garlic (sliced)
1 teaspoon chopped parsley
2 tablespoons lemon juice
4–5 fillets anchovy in oil

Put the olive oil in a saucepan and when hot add 1 pound mushrooms either sliced or quartered. Season with salt and pepper, the sliced garlic, the chopped parsley, and stir well. Now add ½ tumbler white wine, the lemon juice, and 4–5 fillets anchovy in oil. Simmer for 15–20 minutes, and to serve, put the mushrooms on a hot dish, pour a little of the marinade over them and garnish with a few more fillets of anchovy.

Note: This dish is equally nice cold.

Mushrooms Katarina

½ tumbler white wine
1 onion
1 lemon
4 cloves garlic
1 pound mushrooms
mixed herbs
3½ ounces olive oil
salt and pepper
1 teaspoon chopped parsley

Put the oil in a saucepan, add the chopped onion and cook till soft but without burning. Add the sliced garlic, the white wine, the herbs, and season with salt and pepper. Let simmer for 5 minutes. Add the lemon juice and simmer for another 15 minutes. Now add the mushrooms and simmer for 5–8 minutes. When done, put them in another earthenware casserole with their marinade and allow to stand until quite cold. Serve with a little of the strained marinade poured over them.

Aubergines

sherry
aubergines
chilli peppers
oil
flour
eggs
salt and pepper

Peel the aubergines and cut into small pieces. Boil in salted water till tender enough to be rubbed through a sieve. Mix a little flour to this purée of aubergines, and a well-beaten egg, allowing 2 tablespoons flour and 1 egg to every 4 medium-sized aubergines, and 1 tablespoon sherry. Beat thoroughly till quite light, then add salt, pepper, and finely chopped chilli peppers. Drop the mixture, a spoonful at a time, in boiling oil, and fry to a light golden brown.

Chicken and Avocado Salad

3 tablespoons medium sherry
½ pound cooked chicken (diced)
8 ounces canned pineapple (diced)
1 teaspoon lemon juice
mayonnaise
2 generous tablespoons chopped celery
3 avocado pears
salt
paprika

Mix the wine and the lemon juice with the mayonnaise. Stir in the chicken, pineapple, celery, and salt to taste. Thoroughly chill. Just before serving cut the avocados in half lengthways and remove the stones and peel. Arrange lettuce leaves on salad plates and place half an avocado on them. Mix the chicken mixture well and heap in the hollows of the avocados. Dust with paprika.

Pear Salad

1 tablespoon sherry
pears (fresh or canned)
1 tablespoon chopped chives
1 tablespoon sour cream
French dressing
1 packet cream cheese (about 2 ounces)

Blend together the cream cheese and the sour cream, the chopped chives and one tablespoon sherry. Shape into balls. Place half a pear, having taken out the core if fresh, flat side up. Put one of the cheese balls in the cavity and pour over French dressing.

Tomato Salad

white wine dressing (p. 124)
6 tomatoes
hearts of lettuce
3 tablespoons mint leaves
garlic
salt

Slice the peeled tomatoes. Rub the salad bowl with the garlic and salt and place the tomato slices in it with the finely chopped mint leaves. Add a white wine French dressing and toss gently. Serve on the crisp hearts of lettuce.

Potato Salad

1½ pounds potatoes

Ingredients for dressing:

2 tablespoons either red or white wine
4 tablespoons oil
1 tablespoon wine vinegar
1 teaspoon chopped parsley
a little mustard
1 teaspoon salt
½ teaspoon freshly ground pepper
a pinch of chopped chives

(*Note:* it is always advisable to add the dressing while the potatoes are still hot.)

Boil or steam the potatoes, but do not cook so much that they will break. When they are done peel and slice thinly. Put into a salad bowl and pour over the dressing, well mixed previously. The dressing should be thoroughly absorbed by the potatoes.

Watercress Salad

2 tablespoons red wine
watercress
1 tablespoon oil
1 teaspoon mustard
dash of cayenne pepper
salt
sugar

Pour the oil over the watercress. Mix together the wine, mustard and seasoning, stirring well, and sprinkle over the watercress.

Melon with Ginger Wine (*page* 108)

Fruit in Wine (*page* 109)

Puddings, Sweet Sauces and Savouries

PUDDINGS BASED on wine are often extremely easy to prepare, but bear in mind that for this type of dessert the delicacy of the flavour depends on the care taken in using just the right amount of wine and no more. None of these dishes will be improved by overdoing the quantities. Nor will you enhance the natural charm of food cooked in wine if, after a main dish including wine and a wine-based sauce, you then produce a pudding also cooked in wine!

The sweet sauces are useful for brightening up an otherwise mundane sweet dish and the savouries are ideal for completing the meal.

Egg Custard with Chocolate Wine Sauce

4 eggs
1 pint milk
1 ounce sugar
pinch salt

For the sauce:

2 ounces grated chocolate
½ ounce sugar
1 tablespoon ginger wine
½ pint milk
2 level dessertspoons cornflour

Beat the eggs sufficiently to mix the yolks and the whites. Add the milk and a pinch of salt. Strain into a greased pie-dish and stir in the sugar. Bake for about 1 hour on 300°F./Gas 2.

For the sauce: put the chocolate, sugar, wine and most of the milk in a saucepan and heat gently until the chocolate has dissolved. Mix the cornflour to a smooth paste with the remaining milk, add to the chocolate mixture, stir and boil for about 3 minutes. Serve hot.

Sherry Trifle

¼ pint sherry
¼ pound macaroons
2 ounces sponge biscuits
¼ pint custard
1 tablespoon castor sugar
3 ounces sweet almonds
½ pint double cream
apricot or rasberry jam
2 ounces pistachio nuts

Lay the macaroons and sponge biscuits in a glass dish and pour over the sherry and custard; let it stand until the liquor is absorbed. Spread over with jam. Just before serving, whip the cream with a good tablespoon castor sugar and pile on the top of the trifle. Decorate with chopped pistachio nuts and the split blanched almonds.

Zabaglione Meringues

½ cup sweet white wine (e.g. Madeira, Muscatel)
4 tablespoons sugar
4 egg yolks
whipped cream
cream of tartar

Beat egg yolks until thick and yellow coloured. Add sugar and continue to beat until the mixture is thick and smooth. Beat in wine. Cook over hot, but not boiling water, until thick, stirring constantly. Cool over ice, beating all the time with a rotary beater or wire whisk. Refrigerate. Prepare meringue shells by beating the four egg whites with a pinch of salt until they hold a soft peak. Add ¼ teaspoon cream of tartar and ½ cup sugar, beating constantly until thick and smooth. Spread in 2 individual lightly buttered ovenproof dishes. With the back of a tablespoon form meringue into a shell with a deep hollow to hold the filling. Bake in a pre-heated oven (300°F./Gas 2) for 25–30 minutes, or until firm and lightly coloured. Cool.

Watermelon Dessert

sherry
watermelon
½ pound sugar

Cut the watermelon in half and take out the centre and the seeds. Take out all the pulp, put into a basin and half crush it with a fork. Add ½ pound sugar, mix well, and freeze to a mush. The mixture should be sufficiently firm to be eaten with a spoon. Serve in separate glasses and add sherry to taste.

Grapes in Jelly

½ pint white wine
1 pound muscatel grapes
½ pint boiling water
1 orange
1 packet orange jelly
whipped cream
pistachio nuts

Dissolve the jelly in hot water, add the wine and cool. Skin and stone the grapes and put them in individual glasses, but leave some for decoration. As soon as the jelly is nearly set, whip it to a froth and fill individual glasses. Let it set and finish it off with whipped cream, the orange cut in sections and the remaining grapes. Sprinkle with pistachio nuts.

Lemon Cream

1 gill white wine
10 ounces sugar
1 lemon
1 gill water
6 yolks of eggs

Mix the sugar, wine and grated rind of lemon, the lemon juice, and the yolks of eggs in a saucepan, and simmer, stirring constantly, till the cream begins to thicken. Remove from the heat and continue stirring until the cream is cool.

Banana and Walnut Jelly

1 gill sherry
1 gill cold water
3 tablespoons lemon juice
5 tablespoons boiling water
walnuts
2 ripe bananas
¼ pint orange juice
1 tablespoon gelatin
4 ounces castor sugar

Soak gelatin in cold water till soft. Dissolve in boiling water. Stir in sugar and when dissolved, stir in the strained fruit juice and the sherry. Cover a shallow enamelled baking tin with half the mixture. Leave till nearly set. Cover with alternate slices of banana and walnuts 1 inch apart. Cover with remainder of jelly. Allow to set. Chill and cut into small squares. Served piled up in a glass dish or in individual glasses. Decorate with chopped walnuts.

Melon with Ginger Wine

green ginger wine
1 melon
cream (whipped)
ground ginger
preserved ginger

Use a scoop to take out the melon in small balls. Cover with green ginger wine. Top with whipped cream. Sprinkle a little ground ginger on top and decorate with a few slices of preserved ginger.

Stuffed Peaches

½ glass white wine
6 large peaches (not too ripe)
4 small sponge fingers or 2 sponge cakes
sugar
2 ounces sweet almonds including 3 bitter almonds
1 strip candied peel (lemon or orange)

Cut the peaches in half, remove the stone and a little of the pulp in order to make more room for the stuffing. Pound the almonds in a mortar with a little sugar, then put them in a basin, add the peach pulp, the finely chopped sponge cake and the candied peel, also finely chopped. Fill the peaches with the mixture, then put the two halves of each peach together so that they look like one whole one. Put them on a baking sheet, pour the wine over them, sprinkle freely with sugar, and cook in a moderate oven for about 10 minutes or longer, till the sugar has formed a nice crust over them. These can be served either hot or cold.

Fruit in Wine

Here is a pleasant way to flavour wine with fruit.

Skin and stone a peach, apricot, plum and/or any suitable fruit. Cut in several pieces and place in a glass. Pour the wine over it. The wine is drunk during the meal and the fruit, impregnated with several helpings of wine, is delicious to eat.

Syrup for Fresh Fruit Salad

1–2 wine glasses sherry or *Maraschino*
½ pound loaf sugar
½ pint water
juice of 1 lemon

Boil together the sugar, water and the juice of 1 lemon to a thick syrup. When cool add the sherry or Maraschino.

Marmalade Sauce

1 gill sherry
4 ounces granulated sugar
½ pint water
3 tablespoons good quality marmalade

Melt the sugar in a pan with ½ pint water and the 3 tablespoons marmalade. Bring to the boil and reduce to half, skimming when necessary. Add the sherry and reheat.

Sabayon Sauce

¼ pint white wine
2 eggs
¼ pound sugar
1 teaspoon grated orange rind
1 teaspoon grated lemon rind
a pinch of salt

In the top of a double boiler, or in a large bowl over a pan of hot water, beat the two egg yolks slightly. Stir in the white wine, the sugar, the grated orange rind and grated lemon rind, and a pinch of salt. Stir over hot (not boiling) water for about 10 minutes, until the mixture is thick and creamy. Beat the two egg whites until stiff and fold them into the thickened egg yolk mixture. Serve at once.

Coffee Sauce

¼ gill Madeira or *sherry*
2 tablespoons freshly ground coffee
½ pint boiling water
2 ounces lump sugar
¼ ounce cornflour
about 1 tablespoon cold water

Make the coffee in your usual way with the boiling water. Put in 1 tablespoon cold water to send the grounds to the bottom and leave to settle for a few minutes. Then very gently pour off the coffee into a saucepan without disturbing the grounds. Add the sugar. Stir till dissolved. Mix the cornflour to a paste with the cold water. Stir into the coffee. Bring to the boil, stirring constantly. Simmer gently for 5 minutes, then strain into another pan. Reheat without boiling, and add the Madeira or sherry.

Foam Sauce

2 tablespoons Madeira, sherry or *white wine*
4 ounces unsalted butter
1 cup sifted icing sugar
1 beaten egg

Beat butter till creamy. Gradually beat in the sugar, egg and wine. Turn into the top of a double boiler. Beat over water just off the boil, till foamy. Serve at once.

Muslin Sauce

½ gill Madeira or *Marsala*
1 ounce castor sugar
3 egg yolks
1 egg white
small tub single cream (*about 5 ounces*)

Place sugar, cream, egg yolks and egg white in the top of a double boiler. Whisk over water just off the boil, till thick and creamy, then gradually stir in the wine. Whisk again for a moment or two before serving.

Cheese Savoury

3 tablespoons sherry
¼ pound Cheddar cheese
2 ounces butter
pepper
dust of ground mace

Pound the cheese, add the butter and blend well together with seasonings. Place in a glass bowl. Can be served as a savoury for dinner, with biscuits or it may be piped on to croûtons of bread fried in butter.

Parmesan Biscuits

a little sherry
water biscuits
Parmesan cheese
salt and pepper
butter

Take the number of water biscuits required and place on each a heap of grated cheese. Sprinkle sherry on the cheese, a little salt and a good dust of pepper. Put on top tiny bits of butter and place in a tin in the oven till brown. Serve very hot.

Welsh Rarebit

¼ pint dry white wine
1 pound Cheddar cheese
½ pint cream
2 teaspoons Worcestershire sauce
1 teaspoon dry mustard
2 eggs
salt
1 ounce butter

Melt the butter in a double boiler or chafing dish. Add the cheese and stir until it has melted. Stir in gradually the wine and the cream, a spoonful at a time. Blend in the seasonings and then the eggs. Serve at once on hot toast.

Anchovies Menton

sherry
Parmesan cheese (grated)
anchovy fillets
chopped parsley
bread (with crusts removed)
butter
paprika

Fry crustless pieces of bread in butter. Cut them into fingers suitable to take an anchovy. Lay an anchovy on each. Mix the chopped parsley with some grated Parmesan cheese and, with the sherry, make into a paste. Place the fingers of bread with the anchovies in a fireproof dish. Spread the cheese paste over the anchovies thickly. Pour some melted butter on each and grill until brown. Sprinkle with paprika.

Stocks,
Sauces, Dressings, etc.

Wine in marinades

Marinades, which are not always wine-based, are aromatic liquids for improving or 'bringing out' the taste of certain types of ingredients, or in the case of meat, for tenderising, or for preserving food for a period of time before cooking, in much the same way as pickling. Marinades based on wine can, in addition, act as a base for the cooking process and for making sauces.

Note: whatever recipe for marinade you are following, always use a glazed earthenware dish big enough for the ingredients to be properly covered and for them to be turned over at frequent intervals.

General hints on preparing marinades

(1) The length of time that the ingredients are left to marinate depends on the temperature outside (in the summer less time is required).

(2) In the case of either game or meat, cut any pieces that are too big into smaller pieces before placing them in the marinade (this will speed up the process).

(3) Cooked marinades must be brought back to the boil again after two or three days if you intend to continue using them. Take out the ingredients, pour the marinade into a saucepan and bring it up to the boil several times (this takes 3–5 minutes). If necessary, you can make the marinade go further by adding a little wine. Wash out the dish, replace whatever is being marinated, and pour over the marinade *once it has cooled.*

(4) Meat or fish that has been marinated can be cooked in any way you wish (roasted, braised, grilled, fried), but always wipe it carefully after you have taken it out of the marinade, which ever method you are using.

(5) You can also add one or more of the following ingredients to taste, either raw or cooked: a few sprigs of thyme (preferably fresh), a small red pepper, meat broth instead of water (which will make the marinade darker and more aromatic), a tablespoon of kirsch (mainly for venison), neat alcohol (according to taste) or grated orange peel.

Three classic marinades

(1) Uncooked marinade: mainly for terrines, galantines and white meat.

(2) Cooked marinade: for red meat and ground game.

(3) Fish marinade: not to be confused with court-bouillon.

The recipes in this chapter are for these three basic types of marinade. Remember that when cooking with wine you need not adhere strictly to the quantities or proportions given. The amount of wine, oil, onion, herbs, etc. can be increased or reduced according to taste.

Wine in court-bouillon

A court-bouillon, whether or not wine-based, is a highly flavoured liquid intended mainly for cooking various kinds of fish, shell-fish and molluscs. Court-bouillon must always be cooked in advance, for at least 45 minutes over low heat, so that the liquid is properly flavoured.

N.B. although marinades and court-bouillons are closely related in their composition, there is a fundamental difference between them: court-bouillons are only for *cooking* the ingredients, whereas marinades are used to steep the ingredients in beforehand (and very often used as a base for the sauce, too).

Wine in fumets

The word 'fumet' applies only to the cooking of fish. Made from the fish-heads and, if possible, the bones, fumets are used for giving body to fortify fish, soups, fish dishes which must simmer gently on top of the cooker, and, finally, to make fish sauces go further.

Sauces based on wine

According to the eminent French chef Curnonsky, who died in

1956 aged eighty-four, 'wines are the basis of the rich, subtle and delicate sauces that are the glory of French cooking . . . the wide variety of French wines enhances all our dishes'.

The technical details supporting this comment from the '*Prince des Gastronomes*' are these:

(1) the alcohol content in wine not only flavours sauces but gives them a heady aroma, so do not spoil the flavour of a dish by adding too much wine. To ensure the right balance, watch the proportions given in the recipe and taste the sauce frequently. It is not always possible in recipes for exact quantities to be given because so much depends on personal taste (you may like very aromatic sauces, or you may prefer only a slight hint of flavour), and, equally, on how much bouquet the wine has.

(2) the tannin in wine not only gives all dishes, and sauces in particular, an attractive colour: it also acts as an astringent, i.e. it concentrates the sauce. Hence it is almost impossible to ruin a wine-based sauce.

(3) wine flavours dishes, particularly sauces, and gives them a delicious aroma while cooking, so unless the recipe dictates to the contrary, *never hurry* a wine-based sauce.

Although it is unnecessary to supply a separate wine sauce when serving whole dishes based on wine, there are a great many other recipes which can benefit a great deal from the addition of a wine-based sauce. It is often a considerable advantage to be able to prepare a wine-based sauce quite separately from the dish it is to accompany.

Serve the wine sauces with whichever foods you wish: there are no fixed rules, and experimentation with new food-combinations is, after all, the key to the art of gastronomy.

Marinades

For meat:

½ gill port
1 dessertspoon redcurrant jelly
½ gill vinegar
thyme
sweet basil
Worcestershire sauce
1 dessertspoon salt and black pepper (mixed)
marjoram
1 shallot

Melt the redcurrant jelly in a pan and add the port and the vinegar; also a few shakes of Worcestershire sauce. Stir in the mixed salt and pepper, the thyme, marjoram and sweet basil, and the minced shallot. Soak the meat for two or three hours, turning occasionally.

For fish:

1 tablespoon French dry vermouth or *similar Italian dry vermouth*
2 ounces melted butter
½ finely chopped small shallot
1 tablespoon chopped parsley
3 teaspoons wine vinegar
salt and pepper

Mix together the melted butter, wine vinegar, salt and pepper to taste, chopped parsley and the finely chopped shallot. Stir in the dry vermouth.

White Wine Marinade

1 pint white wine
1 tablespoon olive oil
1 tablespoon of white part of leek
parsley
2 cloves
½ pint vinegar
a small onion
2 sliced shallots
1 clove garlic
bay leaf
thyme
4 peppercorns
½ carrot

Fry in a tablespoon olive oil the half carrot, the leek, onion, shallots, garlic, bay leaf, thyme and parsley, cloves and peppercorns. Boil for half an hour in the vinegar and white wine.

Court-Bouillon

2 pints dry white wine
1 pint water
1 chopped onion
1 chopped carrot
1½ teaspoons salt
½ teaspoon thyme
1 tablespoon chopped parsley
1 stalk celery (chopped)
½ bay leaf
10 peppercorns
½ teaspoon marjoram

Simmer all the above ingredients for about 45 minutes, then strain through a fine sieve.

Fish Fumet

white wine or *dry French vermouth*		*fish bones and heads*
	equal quantities	*mixed herbs, to taste*
water		*a few shallots*

Place all the ingredients in a casserole or saucepan, bring to the boil, reduce the heat, and leave the fumet to reduce by about $\frac{2}{3}$. Pass it through a sieve. (Add salt, at the very last minute, *only* if you like very salty food: by the time the liquid has reduced the flavour will already be very strong.)

Basting Sauces

For chicken or turkey:

1. Equal parts of dry French vermouth and salad oil, with salt and pepper to taste.
2. Equal parts dry white wine and salad oil plus a little chopped onion or pressed garlic and a little tarragon or rosemary.

For chicken, turkey, beef, lamb or seafood:

3. Two parts medium sherry, one part soya sauce and one part salad oil—a little chopped garlic if desired.

For beef or lamb:

4. Equal parts of red wine and salad oil, a little onion or garlic, a little rosemary and tarragon.

Marinate in the above sauces for one hour before cooking, and then baste during cooking.

Flavouring Lamb with a sauce

One way of giving a joint of lamb a good flavour is to baste it from time to time with an aromatic preparation obtained by boiling a glass of wine with two finely chopped shallots, fresh thyme or marjoram and freshly ground pepper until it is reduced almost to a purée. This basting, combined with the juices from the meat, will form a natural sauce. No other will be needed.

Bordelaise Sauce

1 gill red Bordeaux
6 minced shallots
3 ounces butter
3 ounces beef marrow
1 lemon
bay leaves
thyme

Put the red wine in a small pan. Add the shallots and cook for a few minutes till it is considerably reduced (to about one third). Add the bay leaves and thyme. On gentle heat add butter slowly, stirring continuously for 5 minutes more. Strain the sauce and just before serving, add the chopped beef marrow with the juice of the lemon. Excellent with steak.

Orange Sauce with Port and Orange Bitters

1 wine glass of port
¼ pound redcurrant jelly
orange bitters

Melt the redcurrant jelly and add the wine glass of port and a dash of orange bitters. This sauce should *not* be thickened.

Tartare Sauce

2 tablespoons dry vermouth or *dry sherry*
½ pint mayonnaise
2 tablespoons gherkins
2 tablespoons stuffed olives
2 tablespoons chopped parsley
1 tablespoon finely chopped onion
1 tablespoon finely chopped drained capers
salt

Mix all ingredients well together. Cover, and to enable the flavours to blend, chill for several hours.

Sauce Espagnole

2 tablespoons Madeira
1 gill white wine
¼ pound butter
¼ pound carrots
2 pounds onions
¼ pound lean gammon
2 ounces mushroom peelings
a few parsley stalks
a sprig of thyme
a small bay leaf
2 ounces flour
3 tablespoons tomato purée
1½ quarts good stock

Cut the vegetables into dice, melt the butter into a saucepan and add the vegetables. Simmer gently until slightly coloured, then add the flour, mix well with a wooden spoon and simmer gently until the flour begins to brown. Then very gradually add the white wine and the stock. Bring to the boil, add the mushroom peelings and the tomato purée, and simmer very gently for 1 hour, skimming carefully as the scum rises. Strain into another saucepan through a sieve, replace on the heat, bring to the boil again and skim most carefully, for the sauce should be entirely free from grease. When finished, the sauce should be reduced to 1 quart. Remove from the heat, add the Madeira, and strain once again. This sauce will keep well in a refrigerator and can be used as required for many dishes.

Sherry and Herb Sauce

¼ pint dry or *medium sherry*
5 tablespoons salad oil
1½ teaspoons Worcestershire sauce
¼ teaspoon salt
½ teaspoon black pepper
1 medium sized onion (finely grated)
1 teaspoon dry mustard
¾ teaspoon mixed dried herbs, i.e. thyme, oregano, rosemary and basil
½ teaspoon garlic salt

Combine all ingredients in a jar and shake or beat well before using.

Orange Sauce

2 tablespoons Madeira, Marsala or *sherry*
2 tablespoons flour
2 ounces butter
¾ pint brown stock
juice of 2 oranges
rind of 1 orange
cayenne to taste
salt to taste

Melt the butter in a saucepan till brown. Stir in flour and when frothy add the salt and cayenne. Stir till dark brown. Add the stock by degrees and, when required, stir in the wine, orange juice and grated orange rind. Serve with duck.

Brown Mushroom Sauce

½ gill Madeira, Marsala or *sherry*
1 pint of brown jelly stock
salt and pepper
1 small can mushrooms
1 tablespoon mushroom liquor

Measure the wine into a saucepan. Add the mushroom liquor. Add the mushrooms chopped finely. Bring to the boil and cook until reduced to half its quantity, then stir in the stock and continue stirring until hot. Season to taste.

Orange Sauce with Port

1 wine glass port
3–4 oranges
pinch of salt
2 teaspoons prepared mustard
½ pound redcurrant jelly
Worcestershire sauce
1 lemon

Grate the rind of the oranges and lemon and mix the juice with all the other ingredients. Allow to stand for a few hours (or all night) and pass through a hair sieve. Add a little Worcestershire sauce. Serve with cold meat or cold duck. *Note:* This sauce will keep some time in a freezer or refrigerator.

Béarnaise Sauce

4 tablespoons white wine
yolks of 3 eggs
6 tablespoons tarragon vinegar
1 tablespoon finely chopped shallots
2 level tablespoons fresh tarragon
1 tablespoon chervil
salt and pepper
½ pound butter
a good dash of cayenne

Put the wine and vinegar in a saucepan with the chopped shallot, the tarragon, the chervil, season with salt and pepper. Bring to the boil and simmer till reduced by ⅔. Remove from the fire and, when lukewarm, add the three yolks of eggs, stirring well. Replace on very low heat (alternatively, keep the saucepan in another saucepan of boiling water), and very gradually add the butter, divided in small pieces, beating with an egg whisk constantly. When all the butter has been used, the sauce should be very light. It should be quickly strained through a conical sieve, then replaced on the heat with a little chopped tarragon, chervil, and seasoned with a dash of cayenne. (*N.B.* This sauce should never be allowed to get really hot. It should be treated as a butter mayonnaise, worked as such, and served lukewarm, otherwise it will curdle.)

Piquant Sauce

1 gill sherry
1 tablespoon tomato sauce
½ pint beef stock
½ tablespoon Worcestershire sauce
2 anchovy fillets

Mix all the ingredients to the beef stock. Boil for 1–2 minutes until it reaches consistency of mayonnaise. Then strain and season.

White Wine Dressing

2 tablespoons dry white wine
4 tablespoons olive oil
½ teaspoon salt
½ teaspoon lemon juice
pinch of dry mustard
pepper
cayenne
onion juice
pinch of sugar

Blend together thoroughly and then chill.

Red Wine Dressing

2 ounces red wine
5 ounces olive oil
freshly ground pepper
½ teaspoon dry mustard
pinch sweet basil
1 ounce wine vinegar
little Worcestershire sauce
pinch tarragon
1 teaspoon sugar

Put the olive oil, the wine vinegar, the dry mustard, the salt and pepper, the red wine, the Worcestershire sauce, the basil, tarragon and sugar into an earthenware bowl. Blend thoroughly and place on ice to chill.

Red Wine and Cheese Dressing

To each cup of red wine dressing add half cup of blue cheese and blend well.

Sherry and Avocado Dressing

4 tablespoons dry or *medium sherry*
¼ pound mashed avocado
2 tablespoons lemon juice
salt to taste
2 tablespoons mayonnaise
¾ teaspoon Worcestershire sauce
¼ teaspoon onion salt
¼ teaspoon celery salt

Blend the avocado, wine, lemon juice and mayonnaise. Add seasonings.

Makes ¾ pint.

A Guide to the Choice of Wines

The following is a suggested list of wines from which to choose when serving a luncheon or dinner.

Hors d'Oeuvres: pale dry sherry or dry Moselle
Melon: young sweet champagne, Madeira, Moselle or ginger wine
Oysters: Chablis, young dry champagne, dry Graves, Pouilly or Moselle
Smoked Salmon: medium dry Graves, hock or Geneva (Dutch) gin
Soup: dry Madeira or sherry
Egg dishes: dry white Burgundy
Fish: champagne, dry Graves, Rhône wines, dry white Burgundy or Moselle
Entrées: red Bordeaux, red Burgundy or Côtes du Rhône
Roast or poultry: claret or Burgundy, or any Rhône wine (such as Hermitage or Châteauneuf du Pape)
Sweets: sweet champagne, Rhine wine, Moselle or Sauternes
Fruit and nuts: sweet Madeira, brown sherry, port, sweet Rhine wine, Sauternes, Tokay

Mulled Wine

(An ideal and much appreciated drink to serve at winter parties.)

3 pints red wine
½ pound sugar
6 thin slices of lemon
thyme
2 bay leaves
3 cloves

Bring the wine and sugar to the boil in a saucepan. Then add the slices of lemon, 1 or 2 sprigs of thyme, the bay leaves and cloves. Remove from the heat at once, set fire to the wine for 1–2 minutes and serve immediately.

Temperatures for Wine

White wines are usually served slightly chilled and red still wines at the temperature of the room. Never add ice to white wines unless serving it in the form of a cup and there is no time to chill it on ice. The right temperatures are:

Dry sherry, French or Italian vermouth
Slightly chilled. Stand decanter for half an hour in refrigerator.

Madeira, Marsala, port and dessert sherry
Room temperature.

White Burgundy, still champagne, Graves, white chianti, white Rhône wine, dry white German wines, white Italian and Spanish wines, Vouvray, etc.
Slightly chilled. Stand in refrigerator for one hour, close to freezing unit, or stand in a pail of ice-water for 20 minutes.

Red Bordeaux, Burgundy, Rhône and Spanish wines, Beaujolais and red wines of the Loire, red Italian and Algerian wines, etc.
Room temperature in chilly weather. At other times at cellar temperatures. Do not stand bottles in hot water.

Sweet French, German, Italian, Swiss and Austrian and other dessert wines
Stand in refrigerator for three hours, or in a pail of iced water for 40 minutes.

Dry sparkling wines
Chill for two hours in refrigerator, or half an hour in ice-water pail.

Sweet sparkling wines
Chill for three hours in refrigerator, or 40 minutes in ice-water.

When wine is required at room temperature, remove the cork when you bring the bottle into the room to allow the wine to breathe. Keep wine in a cool dark place on its side, not upright. Remember that sherry and port will keep perfectly for three or four weeks after opening if corked securely, but low-priced table wines should only be kept for two to three days.

Index